DEC 10, 1941
1ST LANDING
Japanese

CORDILLERA
MOUNTAIN
YAMASHITA'S FINAL
STAND

CAMP O'DONNELL

LUZON

BATAAN
DEATH MARCH
(on FOOT
or RAIL)

TRAIN RIDE

O'DONNELL

PACIFIC
OCEAN

LINGAYEN
GULF

BALI
(US SUBMARINE
AREA

ZAMBALES MOUNTAIN
WHERE TORPIDO
ESCAPED & HID

MANILA
BAY

MANILA

MANILA

Bataan

CORREGIDOR

South
China Sea

CAVITE

VISAYAS

MacArthur
LANDS 1945 BISECTING
The Philippines

CORREGIDOR

Fukodome
Plane CRASH

ENLARGED VIEW LUZON

PALAWAN

KOGA pl
CRASHED

CHINA

KOREA

N

JAPAN

MINDANAO

THAILAND

TAIWAN

VIETNAM

HO CHI MINH
CITY

MANILA

Philippines

DAVAO

Palau
Admirals l
(2 plan ARCHIP
+ Fukodome FLEW
Northwest TO
Philippines to
ESCAPE AMERICAN
ADVANCE

ENCOUNTER
TYPHOON

PALAWAN

PHILIPPINE MAP +
PALAU

SINGAPORE

SOUTHEAST ASIA
MAP

MALAYSIA

Comments

"An unusual story, told from the perspective of a young boy in the Philippines during WWII. The vivid descriptions of one family's struggles during a volatile time provide meaningful lessons about the ways people cope with the unpredictability and savagery of war. The author intersperses historical notes throughout the book and aligns them with the family struggles to illustrate that despite many obstacles, the family as a unit can survive."

~ Teresa Miller, Ed.D., Associate Professor Emeritus, Kansas State University

"Treat yourself to a few hours of first-rate writing. This is solid history wrapped in an engaging story."

~ J. E. Marksteiner, Author and Editor, Fort Myers, Florida

"The author has done a good job in developing his characters…his immediate family and his relatives, which pave the way for the story. The description of WWII and its effect on his family and country makes the reader feel as if they are part of the story."

~ Jerome Biederwolf, Maple Grove, Minnesota

"First-time author Felix Llamido has created a highly readable mix of tender family memoir and fascinating WWII local history of the Japanese occupation of the Philippines. The narrative's pace, combined with vivid imagery, moves the reader through the horrors of war and an extended family's trials and tribulations throughout this tension-filled period.

"The Box of Noli's Bones is great storytelling, punctuated by word pictures that fill all our senses, that juxtaposes a brief historical period with a surprisingly emotional journey."

~ Marc A. Sacher, M.A., Co-founder of Pelican Pens, a Florida Writing Group

"The Box of Noli's Bones is a touching mix of memoir and historical fiction that brings history alive through vivid descriptions of lives caught in war. Juxtaposed with scattered paragraphs of historical accounts, the story provides information readers are likely to find surprising. Many American readers are likely unaware of the historical issues of the Pacific theater of WWII and the involvement of the civilians and soldiers of the Philippines. Personal recollections bring a human face and honesty, highlighting the realities of war. The author's touching early memory of his younger brother, Noli, speaks to the power of the family bond— in war and peace."

~ Dr. Leon Schofield, Clinical Assistant Professor, University of Rochester Medical School

"Much has been written about the US involvement in WWII, but this book is unusual. It takes you inside the Philippines from a young boy's view growing up experiencing this tragic time in history to encounters with the Japanese, details of the resistance efforts, and the battle for day-to-day survival...vivid images of a little boy lying in a meadow watching dogfights to the death between Zero fighters against American P38s until they tumble from the sky, leaving a trail of fire.

"An engaging book!"

~ Gary Brun, Rochester, Minnesota

the Box of NOLI's BONES

By Felix Llamido

ISBN: 9781075938726

Give me ten thousand Filipinos, and I shall conquer the world.
~ General Douglas MacArthur

Many thanks to Elisa Llamido, writer and CEO of Far Star Productions, Inc., for her advice and valuable assistance in editing.

Table of Contents

Table of Images

1-The author, Felix Llamido, age four,
seated right, With cousin Vicenta

Foreword

This is the story of a war that happened in my childhood. As a writer, I am curious.

The book is historical fiction or creative nonfiction. It's a combination of historical facts, relatives and friends memories of the war, and my creative imagination.

If you, kind reader, were to know that the seed of this story sprouted from a food craving, would you read beyond this page?

A college freshman, having never left the confines of his hometown before, eagerly looks forward to coming home for the semester break. Putting his books away, he packs a light suitcase and returns to the familiar surroundings of his childhood.

I was that person more than seventy years ago.

I open my bedroom door to find the penciled markings on the far wall denoting my height and the date when I had it taken with a book atop my head.

There is a faint ink stain on the floor from the spill of the bottle as I was refilling my fountain pen.

That night, I ask Nay, my mother. "Have we any sweet rice? I feel like having some to eat."

My taste buds swell at the pleasant thought of eating this boiled culinary delicacy sprinkled with sugar, topped with grated coconut.

"We do, but they are still in the granary, unhusked. Look for the jute sacks with the red ribbon markings."

The old-fashioned granary is a throwback to the days when we had to store grain apart from the house after the harvest. At an opportune time, the husked rice would be pounded between mortar and pestle to separate chaff from grain before it would be ready for cooking.

Replaced by a direct trip to the rice mill, now the granary sits forlorn, a dark square room, windowless, raised off the ground, closed on all sides to deter rodents.

I push open the door and step into darkness, seeing nothing but obscure shapes. Inside the doorway close to the wall are a garden rake, shovel, and small and large boxes, obviously shoved in haste to be properly arranged at some future date.

I need a flashlight before I can proceed. I shuffle my feet and try to turn in the dark narrow confines.

A box grates rather loudly as it skids from an errant kick of my foot, impeding my line of exit. I have no choice but to pick it up. The contents shift and make a rattling sound. In the light of the morning sun slanting through the open door, I see a marking: NOLI 1942-1944.

I sit on the threshold of that granary, box on my lap, feet dangling in space, mesmerized, not moving. My mind tries to recollect.

Far away, at the end of a dimly lit tunnel in time, I see an image of a baby crawling on the floor, pulling himself up against the side of our sofa until he stands. He lets go, totters and seems about to fall. He takes two steps, and with extended arms grabs the side of the rattan coffee table with his tiny fingers.

That was my brother, Noli, taking his first walking steps

Curiosity overcomes me. Seizing a flat chisel, I pry the lid from the flimsy container not much bigger than a cigar box.

I expect to see an intact skull but instead, only a spoonful of gray dust with fine wisps of hair and gravel-sized particles that probably are bone. There is one long, fully intact bone the size of a chicken thighbone and several flat bones with a slight convexity suggesting remnants of a skull.

My mind is crowded with many thoughts and questions. Why is he here? How old was I when Noli and I used to play together? How old must a child be to acquire the gift of recall?

I resolved that one day I would find the time to piece together memories of my childhood. In so doing, I dug up much more than I bargained for.

Many events begged to be included: the war, things seen, stories heard in conversations with my father and returning veterans, and Noli.

For posterity, I decided to post them all in this narrative.

At the outbreak of the war, I was a two-and-a-half-year-old boy too young to remember. I claim literary license in speaking in the first person of those years, using information I badgered from my elders.

I apologize to historians, military or otherwise. The actual events cited are not intended to be a chronicle of the war that happened in my time, but as a thread to link events in my story, and therefore may not be exactly accurate. I also made assumptions and presumptions, which are figments of my imagination and mine alone.

For the reader who wants to jump to the chapters about the war, I beg your indulgence until you reach the final half of this book.

Felix Llamido

Introduction
December 1941

Two Titans clashed in a place named Pearl Harbor. One fell on his back, surprised by the unexpected assault, roiling the waters with a splash that gathered the momentous force of a malevolent tsunami. Out of control, he rolled across the ocean delivering an offspring, War, to distant shores in the Pacific.

Victims of collateral damage: Guam, Midway, other islands. The Philippines.

"Evacuate!"

The word spread like the dreaded scent of a predator wafting upon a herd of gazelles grazing peacefully on the African veld. The inhabitants of the city of Manila, on the streets, the marketplace, and every household felt a growing sense of dread.

When the Japanese bombed Pearl Harbor on December 7, 1941, at about 9:00 a.m. Hawaii time, people in the Philippines were still in their beds, it being 3:00 a.m. dated the next day. Ten hours later in a synchronized military time table, history books record:

General Masaharu Homma, commanding the 124th Imperial Army of Japan, sent 200 Zero fighters and Mitsubishi bombers to cripple the air attack capability of America in the Philippines by bombing Camp John Hay, Clark Air Base, Nichols Air Field, and Iba Air Base. A large Japanese military force landed on the northern tip of the country at Cagayan and Ilocos provinces.[1]

---

[1] General Masaharu Homma. www.Pacific War.org.av/ Japanese War Crimes/Ten

The succession of attacks on Pearl Harbor followed by the landing of invading forces north and south of Manila and the decimation of the air force capability of General MacArthur's military in the Philippines within the next few days after December 8, 1941, created a ripple effect: damage to infrastructure and railways and mass exodus of civilians and military to safer havens. The US naval fleet deprived of air cover was forced to depart for Java. It left the ground army of Filipino and American troops vulnerable from the air and at sea.

Leaving Manila

Two weeks before the bombing of Pearl Harbor, my aunt Det, then single, paid a visit to our home in Bisal. On her two-hundred kilometer return trip to Manila, she took Nora, my oldest sister, with her for company.

Lured by the thrilling experience of riding the tram for the first time, taking a stroll through the fabled Sunken Gardens along the river where exotic flowers grew in riotous display of vibrant colors surrounded by impeccably cultivated lawns, images of passing vendors on gaily painted pushcarts with tempting ice cream cones, it was too much for a young country girl to refuse.

Because of the approaching Christmas holiday, seeing the bright decorations of Christmas lanterns at night in the glittering city was a pleasure to behold.

My mother, Nay, and I arrived on the train to Manila to bring Nora home. We were to stay a few days before returning in time for Christmas. Left at our home in the countryside in Bisal were Tay, my father; Dida, one of my older sisters; and Tay's young sisters Mari and Esi, both orphaned at an early age and now living with us.

On that fateful day in December, I was roused from sleep by a persistent rough tug on my shoulder. Opening my eyes, still not fully awake, I saw Nora's hand on my shoulder. I turned to my other side and moved away.

"You are a *bangar*," meaning stubborn. "I have been trying to wake you up for the last five minutes. We must leave for home right away. Here are your clothes and shoes."

I made a scowl and was about to resist, when in the background I saw Nay's imperious face, a bowl of food for me in her hand. At the sight and sound of her, I bounded out of bed, and slipped into clothes and shoes in nothing flat. If there was ever a dressing contest, I would have won hands down.

I ate my food and did not even object to the cold, coarse wet towel that was dragged over my face and the combing which followed to plaster my unruly hair neatly parted in the middle.

Nay was a stern disciplinarian who did not stand for any nonsense. Her orders were absolute. Failure at compliance was enforced with a sharp splat with a punishing stick, or the dreaded *kurot,* a sharp twisting pinch expertly applied between thumb and forefinger to the skin on any part of one's anatomy. It was more painful and lasting in intensity than the lash with stick or belt.

Nay had already packed our belongings in a suitcase. We hurried out the door, bidding a parting goodbye to Det. We hailed a passing *calesa,* a horse drawn passenger vehicle, to take us to the Tutuban train station. First, Nay had to haggle for the price of the fare. It was a lesson *Bai* Juana, my grandmother, had taught her children.

We left Det in her living room listening to the repetitious broadcast about the bombing of a faraway place called Hawaii and the admonition to all listening to prepare accordingly. She was going to wait to decide what she should do.

Eight hours later, if she was still listening to the radio, she would have learned of the Japanese bombing of the airbases in the island of Luzon.

We got off the *calesa* a block before the railroad station. Nay espied an open grocery store doing a brisk business with last minute customers. She bought several boxes of matches, a small bag of flour, salt, sugar, candy, and a basket to carry the purchases.

"Here," she looked at Nora, "carry this atop your head and don't lose it." She added, "It is not too heavy for you, I hope?"

We hurried to the waiting train. Already, people, ten abreast, were lined on the concrete platform anxious to climb aboard. Some carried unwieldy hard wooden boxes, which caused angry stares from the people ahead when their backsides were accidentally nudged by the hard corners of these bulky containers.

We were slowly swept along by the moving horde, our position by sheer luck being closest to the side of the train. Nay glanced up at a man sitting by an open window and begged, "Please, sir, I have two children with me. Could you pull them up so we can get inside?"

The man looked at his wife across from him for approval, who scowled back at him, as if to say, of course!

Galvanized into action, the man reached out the train window. Given our light weights, I was easily hoisted in followed by Nora, who, remembering Nay's instructions, hung tenaciously to her basket like a comforting blanket. Nay allowed the moving line to carry her to the train steps, and we were all safely reunited inside.

The old train left the station way behind schedule due to the unusual amount of passengers. Nobody took notice. Even in normal times, it was never on time. It trundled northward like a big fat caterpillar following the lone railway track leading to the city's outskirts.

It entered the open space of fallow land where the breeze, unimpeded by the tall buildings of Manila, felt cooler and noticeably brisk, refreshing the air inside the train's stale compartments. For a moment, people forgot their worries of the war and how it would affect their lives when it came.

Nay tried to keep us occupied by remarking at the passing scenery — green fields cut up in squares by brown mounds of paddies, the mountain looming in the distance, its slope in various shades of green disguising the details of the jungle and vegetation. Nay pointed out a crag silhouetted against the blue sky interrupted by curling white clouds. Didn't that look like the jutting chin of a man in repose at the topmost peak, blowing a smoke of cloud off his puckered mouth?

Tired of staring up, I gazed at the endless flocks of herons inspecting the muddy ground ready to pounce on insects flushed out of hiding by grazing animals. Snow-white herons rode on the mud-covered backs of the domesticated water buffalo, the beast of burden of the Filipino farmer.

After what seemed like hours of stopping at way stations, the train arrived at the town of Tarlac. "This is the end of the line. Everybody must get off," intoned the harried train conductor as he shouldered his way through the length of the train, over and around piled luggage and passengers standing in the aisle. A jabber of questions arose among the passengers who, like us, still had many kilometers to reach their final destinations.

The usual crowd of vendors, who gathered alongside the train selling food, water, and souvenirs through the open windows, provided the answer. "Japanese airplanes just bombed the airbase close by. Some of the bombs destroyed the railway."

Everyone left the train. Home was still a long way to go.

Tarlac Train Station

The empty train reversed course to return to its home base in Manila. Passengers stood on either side of the tracks and pondered their next move. Those living a few kilometers away chose to walk home.

It was already late afternoon. Nay entered the rail station and looked dismayed at the limited space. The building was not built to house a trainload of people. Some of the passengers sought shelter under trees, where at least the air was blowing and not oppressive.

My mother managed to squeeze herself into the middle of the room with Nora and me beside her. A gallant young man rose to offer his seat and space to her, then bowed and elected to find accommodations elsewhere.

Nay laid a blanket on our soft suitcase of clothes by her feet. Laying my head down, I was fast asleep dreaming about ice cream. I was awakened about an hour later by Nora's uncontrollable wheezing. She was perspiring. Each breath started a coughing fit; her face was flushed, the veins of her forehead and neck engorged.

I cried for water and asked for food. Mother hailed a passing water vendor through the open glass window. As she passed us a bottle, the woman appeared deeply concerned for Nora, who struggled to breath.

Nay explained. "She is always like this. The doctor says she has asthma. I forgot to bring her medicine."

"Why don't you let me take her home for the night? I live close by. I have some liniment which might help her." Apparently sensing Nay's unease at letting Nora go with a stranger, the woman added, "I have a daughter about her age. I will send her over to stay with you. Your daughter and I will return early in the morning."

Their eyes met, one mother to another. A message was conveyed.

There wasn't a choice. Nay nodded. "I am sorry for not trusting you."

Nora returned the next morning looking rested and feeling much better. She bragged that not only was she better from the medication, but she also had a bowl of soup for supper, a small slice of rice cake for breakfast, and a cotton blanket and a straw mat to sleep on for the night.

I listened to Nora's narrative with a tint of envy, pouting and crossing my arms, refusing to participate in the conversation.

Nay was effusive with gratitude. She dug into our meager provisions and proffered a slender bar of laundry soap, which the woman, in the time-worn tradition of Filipino hospitality, declined to accept. Nay extracted a promise from this Good Samaritan for her and her family to visit us sometime at our home as guests.

Nay had spent the night sleeping fitfully in a sitting position on the bench she shared with other passengers, mindfully watching over me while I slept comfortably.

We filed out of Tarlac and followed the railroad tracks homeward like a herd of animals following the lead bull. I had never seen the railway from up close before. Its parallel lines of iron seemed to converge into one line several kilometers in the distance as it curved gently to the left or right. The laddered rows of wood beneath the tracks and the crushed rock between offered a geometric pattern that piqued my imagination. Two children slightly older than me, then a third, played a make-believe game of tag as they ran past their parents. With each hour, the hikers dwindled as the lucky ones neared their final destinations.

Alas, for us, there was much more ground to cover.

Nay caught up with me sitting on one of the rails. I had felt some pressure inside one of my shoes. Noting my distress, she put down her load, unfurled the silk scarf from over her head, and sat next to me.

I started to cry and pout and asked to be carried, which Nay ignored. Digging into the pocket of her dress, she held up a piece of red candy the size of a marble. I reached out. Nay held the candy over my head and negotiated.

"I will give you a piece of this if you stop crying."

With that, she cracked the candy in two pieces between her front teeth and handed me half, which I popped in my mouth. She gave me as much water as I cared to drink. She re-wrapped the uneaten candy and put it away, untied my shoes, and examined my tiny feet, making a show of scrutinizing each toe and skin fold.

With her other hand out of my sight, she picked a small pebble off the ground. "No wonder you are hurting. This got inside your shoe." She massaged my feet as she talked, and I gradually felt better.

Nay stood up, retrieved her load, and continued on.

Sleeping in the Open

The third day on the road after leaving Manila, dusk approached as the travelers entered a bend. Nay camped with the children for the night off to one side of the railway tracks in a small clearing covered with short grass recently grazed upon by water buffalo.

She opened the suitcase and dressed Nora and Felix with an extra layer of clothing against the night frost. Around them people filed in and spoke silently, as they huddled with their companions. The veil of darkness descended fast, and the night became still.

Within the hour, everyone slept soundly.

Except for Nay, who grew increasingly concerned.

Would they find food along the way in the stretches of the rail line where there were no people in sight for several kilometers? What about financial resources? Did she have enough to purchase her family's needs? She wondered how much farther the kids could walk. And what about her? She had missed her menstrual periods over the past four months and her belly seemed fuller.

Pulling her shawl about her, her hand brushed against the rosary beads around her neck. She fingered them and prayed. Midway through her meditation, she nodded and fell into a dreamless sleep.

The next day, Nay set a pace with purpose and will. She planned a game rewarding her children with a hug or a morsel of food and fruit for a certain distance traveled.

She considered it a good omen that the local inhabitants offered fruit, cake, and water along the way in return for a few centavos.

By mid-afternoon, Nay started to sense moments of despair. In a few hours, it would again be dark. Silently, she implored her two children, who followed obediently like chicks to the mother hen, to keep up the pace.

Her head swiveled first to one side of the tracks then to the other, as if in search.

Of what?

The Hut of Salvation

Nay saw it in the last glimmer of the setting sun on the horizon, a tiny prick of yellow light off to her left, not far away. It became sharper as darkness enveloped the countryside.

Without star or moonlight, she unerringly led her brood in a straight line, walking through the rice paddies that, thankfully, were not muddy at this time of year. They came upon a small hut fenced by overgrown shrubbery.

Nay hailed in a loud voice, "*Ma Ma, Na Na,*" madam, sir. In the stillness of the night, her voice sounded like the bleating of a lost lamb looking for its mother.

A man emerged from the hut, an oil lamp swinging on his outstretched arm, as he scanned the darkness. He appeared relieved to find Nay and two children, not an obvious threat.

Nay spoke plaintively. "We are tired and hungry and we seek shelter."

He did not hesitate. He pointed to the gate inviting them to enter. A woman came by his side holding a baby. Nay explained her family's situation.

The hut was small, roofed with sheaves of dry cogon grass, and nipa-palm-thatched walls. It had an opening that rendered entry but no door or curtain, which made it possible for Nay to see the lamplight from the rail tracks. It was raised on bamboo poles three feet off the ground with bamboo slats for a floor, devoid of any furniture. A clay pot of water with a dipper made of coconut shell on a wood handle sat in the corner.

Empty coconut shells for plates and an empty pot, obviously from an interrupted supper due to our arrival, lay on the floor.

Nay knew before entering the hut that there was no room for the three of them. She had been in grass huts of farmers before. There was barely space for the husband, wife, and baby to sleep.

It intrigued her. What brought her here, to this place?

Andoy and Iska

"We do not have space for you to sleep inside as you can see." The farmer pointed toward the hut. "But my wife will cook you something to eat, and I will go and prepare a shelter in the yard." He reached for his *bolo*, sheathed on its scabbard hanging on a peg by the door, and disappeared into the night.

Iska, his wife, laid her sleeping baby—wrapped in a threadbare cotton rag, once white many laundry washings ago—in a corner. She placed a pot of rice on the stove. She added ginger, salt, and slices of papaya and malungay leaves—retrieved from plants grown around the perimeter of the yard—to a pan of boiling water.

Iska cut two banana leaves to cover the bare bamboo floor and placed the pots of cooked food in the center.

Nay and her children washed their hands with water from the clay pot and ate hungrily with bare hands. It was a feast, even for Felix, who disliked vegetables. They went outside in the dark, bellies full.

Andoy, the farmer, had placed a bamboo pole horizontally at head height between two tree branches and leaned sticks against the pole. Cut palmetto leaves made a crude roof with banana leaves on the bare ground to lie on. Iska came to help Andoy finish the temporary shelter.

Nay again wondered what made her travel to this place. She felt the gentle nodding of the children at her side as they struggled to stay awake.

"I am grateful for what you are doing for us. With my children and our load, it has been difficult to make good time having to stop frequently. I am no longer sure if we can ever make it home before the Japanese soldiers arrive."

Something seemed to rustle in her ear, as in a whisper.

It prompted her to ask, "Do you know of anyone around here who has a *calesa* or motor car for hire so we can finish our journey?"

Andoy, lighting a dry stick off the oil lamp to start the fire on a pile of wood next to our shelter, shook his head. "I am afraid not. We don't travel much outside the farm…"

Iska's head turned in Andoy's direction. "What about Taba?"

Excited by the news she had heard, Nay did not rest well that night. Before daybreak, she stirred the embers to light the fire, packed their belongings, and cajoled Nora and Felix to wake up.

Leaving a few silver *pesetas* on the threshold of the hut for the farmer, they headed back to the railway tracks to rejoin the rest of the travelers.

A woman with a child about Felix's age sidled up to Nay. In conversation, Nay mentioned that they had a lead on a possible conveyance to get home.

Iska had said, "There is a man with a car. I only heard of him by the name of Taba. Go back on the tracks, head north, and walk until you come to a dirt road that crosses the rails. Then, go left. It will take a man walking at a normal pace time to finish smoking two cigarettes to reach his place."

-o-

There is a common saying. "If you want to keep something a secret, don't tell anyone." Before the road crossing was reached, one yokel told another yokel until a passel of interested travelers stuck to Nay like fleas on a dog's back.

The Motor Car

The trail was a fluffy powder of ankle deep dust the color of caramel, devoid of rock or gravel. When the rains came and water reached the knees, this low flat road this would become an almost impassable river of mud, as animal and wheeled traffic churned the water and dust into the consistency of gruel.

The straggly travelers pulled into the yard in tired groups of twos and threes. It wasn't difficult to find. Tire tracks led to his driveway.

The surprised man and his wife watched us enter the yard from his shaded balcony. He descended the stairs.

I then saw why the man, Andres, was called Taba, which means "lard." His belly stuck out like a large watermelon. It jiggled when he laughed. His legs were incongruously short, a birth anomaly that made it impossible for him to reach the accelerator with the toes of his foot, which was why he had strapped a four-inch-thick block of wood to the pedals of the motorcar.

Taba offered free access to the deep well where a pail on a rope lay close by. After each of us had our fill of water, someone spoke in everyone's behalf requesting transportation to our final destinations. He glanced at his wife for help and looked at the three children among the group.

Silently counting heads, he apparently could not resist the temptation to earn a few more pesos in what could be a long war ahead. He nodded in approval.

"But I will need your help."

Andres told us, "When news of the Japanese invasion reached my ears two days ago, I hid my car behind the house beyond the pigpen camouflaged by a bamboo grove, dried brush, and hay.

Now only the telltale signs of the tire tracks showed. But within days, once it got covered by the fast-growing grass, no one would guess it was there.

An old model car sat on hollow blocks devoid of its four tire wheels. It had front and back seats, long running-boards, sloping front fenders, and a hard top.

The men helped Taba retrieve and install the tires; the buried hand crank was unearthed not far away. Now fully assembled, they wheeled it to the front yard, where Andres brought the car back to life after a few cranks on the engine.

Four adults filled the back seat. Three children climbed in next and remained standing. Three adults sat on the front seat, making ten passengers inside the vehicle.

Luggage was strapped on the back and roof, plus a spare can of gasoline. Four men stood on each running board, holding onto the ledge of the car roof.

Two adults sat on the sweeping front fenders holding on to a jury-rigged rope strapped across the engine cowl.

The car wheezed sideways and forward, traveling at a sedate ten miles per hour at top speed due to the age of the car and the enormity of its load.

The road was not macadamized, just a primitive road blazed out of forest and rough terrain. The main road was leveled land with a foundation of large rocks, some bigger than a man's head, washed down the mountain from beds of nearby streams.

To smooth the jutting points of the rock base, the road builders threw in gravel. The rainy season washed the gravel away, baring the irregular rocks beneath.

Lack of timely maintenance made a journey through such roads daunting with the possibility of a blown tire or broken axle for the careless driver.

-o-

The passenger load lightened every few kilometers by those fortunate enough to live in homes close by. We were thankful for more sitting room.

By late afternoon, we rode along the street of Bisal, our hometown. Nay, Nora, and I were the last passengers to reach our destination.

Home Arrival

I knew we were home when I saw Teriong's everything store, where one could buy candy displayed in large jars, cigarettes, rice, vinegar, charcoal for the flat iron, and rice bran for the pigs.

Ahead stood the whitewashed façade of the town hall with the flagpole in front, followed by the free flowing artesian well gushing sweet, clear water day and night from an underground spring.

I could guess what I would see next: the elementary and intermediate school buildings and the lush green lawn of Bermuda grass in the yard where my friends Benny, Filo, Munar, and I love to romp, wrestle, and play.

The motor car stopped at the crossroad to a familiar lane. It led to our home in the bend yonder, where a cluster of trees hid it from direct view. I jumped off the motor car and ran, forgetting to carry my assigned load, eager to stretch my legs.

I opened the latch to enter the yard. Five barking dogs dashed to greet me at the gate. Barks changed to yelps, and bounces almost knocking me down.

Betty, with the incongruous name for an alpha male, licked my face and hair. Guardia, the female, and her three puppies now fully grown, all fiercely loyal guardians of our home and yard, took their turns mushing me up. Following the pecking order of dog hierarchy, Tigla, the youngest, greeted me last.

Nay and Nora caught up with me at the pergola adorned with flowering vines crowning the arches. We were welcomed by Dida, my second older sister, and Anday, Dida's godmother.

Both beamed with relief at our arrival. Nay looked around for Tay, Esi, and Mari, who were conspicuously absent, then at Anday, whose expression became serious.

"*Ay, comare!*" she lamented. "I am glad you are home at last. A lot of things have happened in your absence. That is why I am here with Dida."

Anday took the load of luggage from Nay's hand and led her to the pergola seat. Nay removed her shoes, revealing the rime of several days of dust displayed prominently in contrast against the pale skin of her covered feet. Anday went inside the house and returned with a jug of water. She took one of Nay's feet off the ground, placed it on her lap, and gently massaged it.

Dida and Nora went up the stairs to prepare supper, while Dida pumped Nora with endless questions about what it was like to live in the city.

Anday then began to tell her story.

2-Bai Juana's ancestral home and Felix's place of birth.

Mangalem Market Day

(Anday's Story)

Seventy thousand years ago, an underground volcano located ten degrees below the equator in the torrid zone of the tropics spewed tons of molten lava upwards that cooled off and jelled, building a huge mountain. An archipelago was born out of its many peaks that rose from the sea creating the islands of the Philippines. The largest island to the north became Luzon, where I was born and raised.

A town called Mangalem grew at the foot of this large mountain. It is the ancestral home of Juana, my widowed grandmother, who resided with her eldest daughter, Concha, and Concha's husband, Melchor.

Anday told us of the morning a few days earlier, the same day when Nay, Nora, and I were on the train trying to head for home.

My two orphaned aunts Mari, 10, and Esi, 12, had arrived an hour earlier on foot, from our home in Bisal five kilometers away.

They chatted animatedly with *Bai* (grandmother) Juana as they headed in the direction of the church. The church ground had become the popular venue for fiestas and market days; this was market day. Each carried a bamboo basket in the crook of their arms.

They were aware that a war had started, with news of an invading Japanese force landing to the north and reported bombing of military airfields in the island of Luzon earlier that day. Everyone

26

felt it would take a few days longer for the Japanese soldiers to pass the nearby towns. It still exists today.

So what if the conflict happened? They had never been involved in a war before. Where would they go?

Bai Juana outlined the plan for the day. The two girls were assigned to buy the dried fish and fresh vegetables on the far side of the market. *Bai* would head for the meat and fresh fish section close by. Panning the crowd of shoppers, she anticipated that butchered meat would be in short supply that day

.

3-Bai Juana, Felix's grandmother, October 15, 1940

She reached into her waist, took out a coin purse tied to the drawstrings of her long skirt, and spilled a few coins into the girls' open palms. They would all meet in an hour. *Bai* pointed with her nose and pursed lips to an open area close to the middle of the convent porch by the large wood pillar.

27

The crowd seemed to be in a jostling mood that day, *Bai* thought. Perhaps it is the news of impending war in the air.

The sight of fresh vegetables in pleasing shades and colors lightened her mood. Neat piles of purple eggplants, red tomatoes, green string beans, green bitter ampalaya fruit, and malungay leaves lay on the ground where vendors had spread bright colored squares of cloth.

Esi knelt and nimbly snagged a pile of large tomatoes to her chest before haggling for the price, while Mari raked in several eggplants with the deftness of a gambling croupier. Both haggled with the vendors to lower their prices, then paid the negotiated few centavos, and moved to the next items on their shopping list.

Jubilant at accomplishing their assigned tasks quickly, they headed for the appointed meeting place.

Bai Juana's shawl was spread on the grass, staking space from other shoppers. Mari and Esi knelt on the ground facing her. *Bai* looked at their loaded baskets and nodded in approval.

"Three of those eggplants go to your house; these two tomatoes are for me to take to Concha's…"

A droning sound with the intensity of a million angry bees interrupted the still air. The silhouette of an airplane with a red circle on each side of its fuselage swooped down from the sky.

-o-

A Japanese pilot at the cockpit had just finished a surprise raid with his squadron attacking the parked military aircraft at the nearby Air Force base.

He was elated with his personal score: one of his bombs destroyed an American fighter plane; two others on the ground had caught fire.

As his squadron returned to base in the north, he noticed he had a few rounds left in his machine gun.

He recalled that his squadron commander had ordered every pilot to expend all bombs and bullets, confident that all enemy air power had been neutralized from the surprise attack they had just inflicted. He espied the large knot of people milling like ants below and nosed his plane downward.

The guns continued to fire until the magazines emptied before he turned back to rejoin his group.

Actually, the bullets landed harmlessly on the outlying hills beyond and hit no one.

-o-

The unfamiliar roar of the Japanese warplane and the gunfire that ensued peeled back the flimsy veneer of calm among the people who thought the war was many days away before it would affect their lives.

"The Japanese are here…they just fired upon us…we are going to die…oh God, save us…"

"Let's run this way… no, let's go that way."

The resulting stampede of hundreds of people scurrying in all directions fueled a growing panic. Many headed for the door of the convent to find safety within the thick brick walls of the old church.

The small back door, which could only admit two people abreast at a time, perhaps three if they were skinny, caused a bottleneck. More pushing and shoving nudged the upright wooden pillar supporting the middle porch of the convent.

Some carpenter must have thought that if the heavy weight of the convent was downward, then there was no need to buttress the post laterally from sliding off.

Whoosh!!! Thud!!

It happened so fast and with such force that the fallen post made an indentation on the soft ground.

Bai Juana was still kneeling on her haunches, right hand extended, task almost finished, when the pillar fell between her and the two girls. She lay on her side, stunned, staring at the whitewashed log mere inches from her face. Her right hand was pinned beneath the log.

At the moment before impact, Mari and Esi had jumped aside, lucky to be unscathed.

They noticed *Bai*, ashen faced, on the other side trying to extricate herself. They screamed.

People around them stopped running and came to help lift the log; others carefully moved *Bai* away. Her mangled right hand dangled helplessly by her side. Relieved of the pressure, her hand began to bleed in spurts. They wrapped the injured limb with her scarf. When it bled through, someone ripped a strip of cloth from the bottom of her ankle-length skirt. The new reinforcing bandage, now tighter than the first, stemmed the bleeding.

The priest was summoned. He said a prayer and took charge. "She has to get to a doctor!"

This was not possible. The only doctor in town had been ordered to proceed to the closest hospital seventy kilometers away. Under a contingency plan formulated years before in anticipation of a war by the military authorities, medical facilities in the province were to be closed. Only selected hospitals close to the theater of war were to remain open in anticipation of casualties.

A helpful man carried *Bai* Juana to her home, as Esi and Mari sprinted ahead. Melchor and Concha rushed out into the street and viewed *Bai*'s condition in disbelief. They carried *Bai* up to the house and laid her on the bed. Before leaving, the man reached into his belt pouch, pulled out several folded betel leaves, and pressed them in *Bai*'s uninjured left hand.

Bai recognized what it was, took one of the leaves in her mouth, and began to chew. Inside this pungent leaf were ground areca nut and a smidge of white lime. Called *gagalen*, it was a commonly chewed concoction among the older people and farm folk to make the drudgery of long hours of hard work bearable.

It made her feel relaxed and lethargic.

Concha and Melchor spoke in urgent whispers. What were they going to do? Managing her by themselves at home was not an option. A mangled hand could get infected and become fatal.

They came up with a plan to get her to a hospital, even if it entailed carrying her on foot.

But, they would need Tay's help. Esi and Mari were to remain in Mangalem should their help become necessary.

Melchor was already a man in his late forties, thus was not a conscript in the Philippine army. He was in good physical shape, having been conditioned to work with the Forestry Service for years hiking up to the mountain station to monitor plants and trees. His sinewy calves and thigh muscles were well developed from numerous treks on mountain trails often carrying a heavy load on his *sakupit,* a rattan woven backpack strapped to his shoulders, for hours without a break for food or drink.

For his trek on foot to Bisal, he loaded a much lighter weight on his back containing two days of food and a small canteen. Water was readily available in clear springs along the way if one knew where to look.

The five kilometers on the flat terrain was an easy dog trot for Melchor. He reached and crossed the river and looked in consternation at the flurry of activity on the main street of Bisal. Is there a festivity?

He saw the loosely assembled soldiers, and he knew.

Muster Time

(Anday's Story Continues)

News of the upcoming war came through the only available working radio in the town of Bisal, at the home of its most illustrious inhabitant, Don Toribio. Following his routine, he got up that morning, careful not to rouse his sleeping wife, put on his slippers, and silently padded to the living room.

Toribio reached overhead to turn on the battery-operated radio on a shelf against the wall. He expected to hear the opening song "South of the Border" on his favorite radio program.

Instead, he heard the oft repeated broadcast that had taken over the airwaves. Japan had bombed Pearl Harbor at three o'clock in the morning Manila time, and now, at eight o'clock, the Japanese had bombed five military targets in the Philippines.

He turned up the volume and called the servants for coffee and breakfast.

There was a repetitive appeal for all military units to form and await further orders. The Don summoned Bolol, his head vassal, to spread the message through the *Sistema*. It was one of several forms of communication which, he, as ranking military officer in the town, had formulated with the fellow army reservists under him, to follow at a time like this.

Bolol saddled a horse and headed one kilometer away to Miano's home. That was all he had to do. Miano now would inform his two closest neighbors who were reservists themselves, and they would inform the next person down the line. It had worked in a trial run when a farmer needed helping hands to harvest his rice field.

My father, Tay, was feeding the chickens and planned to clean the goat pen, when he heard the dogs bark. A man dressed in military uniform waited outside the fence.

It was Barok, his school janitor also in the army reserve. He knew the man would not come to his house unless it was through the *Sistema*.

Tay was taken by surprise at the unexpected news given to him. He thought about his wife and two children still in Manila. He took a small measure of comfort in knowing Nay's level headedness.

Nay, ever resourceful, would find a way to bring Nora and me to a safe place and bring us home.

There was one other problem. His two sisters, Mari and Esi, had gone to Mangalem for market day. They were not expected to return until later in the day. He was left to take care of the house and animals and my sister Dida, age six.

He walked to his nearest neighbor's house a quarter of a kilometer away.

-o-

Anday was a middle-aged woman married a few years to a much older man; they had no children. She was godmother to Dida. Of course, she was willing to help. She would sleep over to keep Dida company and tend to our dogs, chickens, and goats until Nay's return.

On the main street of Bisal, in his khaki uniform crossed at the chest with two bandoliers of rifle ammunition and wearing a hard-brimmed leather army hat, Tay seemed transformed as he cut a warrior's profile with his lean build, high cheekbones, and piercing stare.

Pinned at his lapel were the gold bars of a first lieutenant. At his side rested his army issue bolt action rifle, a weapon he fastidiously maintained. He faced Don Toribio, his friend, now his commanding officer, Captain Toribio, and awaited instructions.

Coming from different directions toward them was a growing assembly of uniformed soldiers who had left home and family to go to war. Surrounding them were assorted horse-drawn *carromatas, carabao*-pulled carts, and two Model T Fords, all civilian conveyances commandeered to transport the company's supplies.

It was a ragtag, hastily assembled army unit.

4-Tay, Felix's father, May 31, 1940
Written in his own scroll on the back, "Lieutenant, Philippine Army."

Hospital Trip

(Anday's Story Continues)

Tay saluted his superior officer, Captain Toribio, and did an about face while unbuttoning his shirt flap to retrieve his notepad and pencil. He scanned the soldiers in search of the company master sergeant.

He recognized a familiar figure with a distinct loping dogtrot in the background weaving his way toward him from the direction of the river. Melchor disappeared fleetingly amid the growing throng, emerging in front of a Model T Ford being loaded with provisions, folding tents, and ammunition.

Melchor held up his hand. Tay nodded, signaling him to approach. Melchor's grave countenance and urgent strides sent a sense of foreboding in Tay's chest. Dispensing with pleasantries, Melchor delivered the bad news about *Bai* Juana.

Tay knew he was caught between the horns of a dilemma. He knew what must be done, but now that he was in the Army, there were rules to abide by. He conferred with his commanding officer.

Toribio and Tay were friends and had become godfathers to each one's sons. They went on campouts and hunting trips together, attended important weddings of common friends. At social gatherings in town, it was unthinkable for a host to invite one without the other. Captain Toribio conveyed to Tay the fact that although the orders were clear to join the military force building up in Bataan, there appeared to be no sign of immediacy of the impending war.

They listened to the buzzes of conversation among the waiting men, sharing local news like who died, who got married, and the recently mired water buffalo in the muddy quicksand just outside of the town. There were still a few men who had not yet arrived because of slow travel on foot from outlying farms.

The captain made a snap decision. "Get Juana to a hospital. Isco, who lives across the river, is supposed to be here with his horse and *carretela,* but has not yet reported. On my orders, have him take you and Juana in his vehicle to the doctor."

He gave Tay the coordinates of the company's final destination in Bataan on a piece of paper and urged him to catch up with them at best speed. "Wear your uniform and carry your rifle at all times. I will write your marching orders which might help in case you get stopped along the way by military police."

Tay turned to Melchor. "I will come with you. Before we leave for Mangalem, I would like to go home once more to tell Anday of this new development. Hopefully, she won't mind staying over to care for Dida at my house until Mari and Esi return."

End of Anday's Story

Bai Juana lost her mangled right hand. It had festered, leaving the doctor no alternative but to amputate at mid-forearm.

Following Bai's discharge from the hospital, Tay and Melchor accompanied her to Mangalem. On their way, the Philippine soldiers allowed them to pass because of Toribio's letter. But they commandeered Isco, his horse, and the *carretela*.

They entered a forest where Melchor's woodsman skills came in handy. With his sharp *bolo*, he felled two bamboo trees, cut them in long strips, and wove them together with rattan vines. Next he cut two carrying poles that Tay and Melchor hefted onto their shoulders to transport *Bai* in the makeshift gurney through the rough terrain.

They saved a day of travel by portaging *Bai* through narrow trails and fording shallow streams over jungle paths known to Melchor. Ten days later, they were back home in Mangalem.

Bai's bandages were removed each day, the wound cleaned with soap and water. Soiled bandages were washed, rinsed in boiling water, hung to dry in the sun, and reused.

Mari and Esi cared for *Bai* in this manner until her wounds started to heal. They then rejoined the family in Bisal.

Anday paused. Her chronicle of recent events in Nay's household was over. She looked at the moonless sky and sighed, relieved of her burden. Peering into the darkness, she searched for

Nay's face in the direction of utter silence, then reached for Nay's folded hands, now wet with tears.

Frogs croaked, cicadas buzzed and clicked, crickets chirped as they began their nocturnal mating calls. It was as if they were saying, "You have been talking for hours and we have not intruded. Now it is our turn."

Attempt to Rejoin the Company

Tay was determined to rejoin his military unit and Captain Toribio. He felt honor bound to pay a debt to a longtime friend who may have stretched the rules a bit to save *Bai*'s life.

In the days spent taking *Bai* to the hospital, Tay had assumed that the advancing Japanese army could already be close to their doorstep. If that was the case, then the usual inland route to Bataan would not only be impassable but dangerous.

Tay did not know that the enemy was also encountering logistical difficulties of its own. Transporting men and materiel on mountainous terrain also delayed their timetable.

He consulted his pocket map. Bataan lay southwest of his current location and did not seem that far away. What if he followed the mountain south until it tapered at Mount Natib to Bataan peninsula? On foot, it could be reachable in a few days, give or take.

He discussed his plan with Melchor, who listened wordlessly. He could not blame Tay for trying.

"It is possible," he replied. He looked directly into Tay's face. There is a caveat for such a journey. One must know how to live off the mountain and know how to cope with Mother Nature's caprices. The mountain could be a harsh place. Melchor, being a mountaineer, knew this and counseled Tay. It was fruitless to try dissuading Tay.

Three weeks later, Tay was back in Mangalem, visibly thinner. *Bai* Juana beckoned him to a seat next to her reclining chair.

Tay took the back of her left hand and pressed it to his forehead in the traditional show of greeting and respect for an elder.

Looking at *Bai*, he felt inwardly elated at her physical condition. The stump of her right forearm showed a faint blood ooze and yellowish scanty suppuration through the bandages, but it was draining, not building up inside the amputation site, a good sign.

Concha came out of the kitchen with a hot plate of food. Ravenously, Tay wolfed down his meal. Everyone gathered around and waited.

A basin of water to wash and a clean dishrag for his hands. A soft belch. Tay leaned back in his chair and began his story.

At the onset, he had no trouble walking along the trail leading to the foot of the mountain in the early dawn. Before the sun rose and the air warmed, he entered the forest where he traveled in shade and found streams with good drinking water and abundant fish and eel. He loaded up on provisions, then salted and dried fish for a day before starting up the mountain.

Tay reached the spine of the mountain and found the foot trail described to him by Melchor. His spirits were buoyed the first few days by the fast pace he was able to keep; at the rate he was making time, he felt confident he would be in Bataan in a week.

Then fickle weather intervened. It started to rain, a faint drizzle at first, then a downpour. The wind came in gusts. Dark clouds blotted out the sun. The wet shrubs and waist-high *cogon* grass brushed at his body mercilessly, basting him with rainwater, until he chattered from the cold, his raingear of no use.

Walking up the slippery wet grass became slow and treacherous. Mud caked on the soles of his boots in sticky layers, making them heavier with each stride.

He found a rock ledge under which he sought shelter. There was a small cave that he chose not to enter for fear of a predatory animal or a snake, which he detested.

He fished into his pockets and came up with a soggy box of matchsticks; thus, he was unable to light a fire.

Without warning, there was absolute darkness. Day had turned to night. It was an intimidating experience. He heard the noise of frogs and crickets, but he could not see. The rain did not let up for three solid days, forcing Tay to stay in place. Clearly, he did not anticipate the magnitude of the obstacles Melchor had tried to warn him about on the mountain.

Cold and wet, he felt discouraged. He had been on the hike for several days, and now he was bogged down by the inclement weather. Bataan seemed farther away than when he started his journey.

He also needed to re-provision. The days of delay from the heavy rains had depleted his food supply. One more day, he decided; tomorrow he would make a decision on what to do.

Tay awoke, racked with fever, body aches, and a hacking cough. He remembered Melchor's advice: "If you ever get sick in the high altitude with these symptoms, get off the mountain!"

He did not know or remember how he found his way back to Mangalem. He came across an animal trail, lost it, picked up another, and realized he was back up the mountain again. Delirious and hungry, he walked in an aimless pattern of circles.

A hard, cold, gusty wind came suddenly as though it was going to rain again. It propelled him forward like a force behind a sail. He could not resist it, for as he tried to go the other way, he stumbled. His face felt warmer as though facing the sun, yet it was almost dusk.

In the waning hour before the sun dipped beyond the mountain crest, he trudged on like an automaton putting one foot in front of the other, his senses dulled. He heard the familiar sound of gravel of the riverbed beneath his feet. He had finally found the footpath leading back to Mangalem and followed it to Melchor and Concha's home.

"And here I am."

He looked down feeling disappointed. He had tried to join his friend, Toribio, and had failed.

Bai's Bargain

Bai reached into a covered dish on the side table, took a fold of *gagalen* and popped it into her mouth. As she chewed, the pungent mixture soaked between her cheek and gum. A feeling of stupor and euphoria started to flow through her, obtunding the throb on the fingers of her missing right hand, a phantom pain experienced early on after an amputation.

She wrapped her arm with a soft flannel cloth and closed her eyes as if about to fall asleep. In point of fact, she was digesting what Tay had said.

Softly, she said, "I am grateful for the sacrifice you have made to get me to the hospital. I owe you my life. It is unfortunate that you were unable to rejoin your unit, despite your trying.

"But, let me ask you this," she continued. "In the few weeks since the war began, there has been news that the war is not going well for our side. Assuming that you were able to reach Bataan, with all the commotion, what is the probability of finding where your unit would be?"

It was Tay's turn to speak, "You are right. The odds would be low. Battle lines shift as ground is gained or lost."

Probably thinking she was asleep, he rose and tiptoed quietly from the room.

In the stillness of her bedroom, *Bai*'s eyes suddenly flickered open a few minutes later. She murmured in the direction of the religious icon hanging on the wall.

"My hand! You took my hand in exchange for sparing the life of my daughter's husband! Was that the bargain?"

She had no doubt what her answer would be. She began to pray, and ended, "I accept the bargain, willingly."

And she said it again. "I accept. Thank you, Lord."

5-Bai Juana, 1947
She lost her right hand in 1941 at the onset of the war.

The March out of Bisal to Bataan

On December 24, 1941, General Douglas MacArthur, realizing that America would be unable to extend assistance for the defense of the Philippines due to the losses at Pearl Harbor, invoked War Plan Orange, a sort of Plan B. Japan had forced this decision by launching the surprise attack crippling the military capability of the Philippines bombing its planes and airfields scant hours after the sinking of the American ships of war in Hawaii.[2]

Captain Toribio's men, fully assembled, finally left Bisal. They marched three abreast, weapons slung smartly on their shoulders as if on parade, out of town to join other units for Bataan. Children, men too old to go to war, womenfolk, dozing babies on their hips, watched the passage with more than passing interest. Young boys marched alongside trying to keep up with the longer strides of the soldiers. Some carried wooden sticks for toy rifles on their shoulders, emulating the soldiers for a few yards before returning to their families.

The soldiers commandeered carts, cars, and *carretelas* to carry the heaviest equipment. Despite this, the men felt the weight of their rifles on aching shoulder muscles. Men shifted their weapons to various carry positions, no longer caring about the prescribed manner of proper marching. The officers, themselves spent, did not object as long as the growing procession kept moving. Conversation was reduced to a minimum to conserve energy.

[2] War Plan Orange-Wikipedia. www.history.army.mil/books, wikipedia.org, Bataan Death March-World War II. History.com, Wikipedia.org/Battle of Corregidor/Gibraltar of the East, Wikipedia.org/Corregidor#Geology

On the fourth day, the company passed through the first of several lines of resistance. American and Philippine soldiers in freshly dug trenches manned a variety of cannons and machine guns meant to delay the advance of the Japanese force that had already landed at Lingayen Gulf. The weapons pointed in the direction from which Toribio's group had come.

Local vendors mingled with the soldiers as if they were at a carnival selling iced bottles of San Miguel beer. Some soldiers were shirtless, soaking up the sun, smoking cigarettes that dangled from their lips.

A lot of waving and good-humored conversations were exchanged, but the tension was palpable. One wonders how many of these men entertained the possibility they might never pass this way again; they could be captured or killed.

The exodus of soldiers ended in the thumb-like projection of Bataan peninsula. They came in an endless stream from various directions like flocks of sheep being herded within the protective gates of a corral. Surrounded on three sides by water and a mountain on the fourth, their position appeared formidable. In the water, a tadpole shaped island named Corregidor and other lesser islands named Caballo, El Fraile, Carabao, all bristled with cannon and various weapons of war.

Military strategists felt that they should be able to defend themselves for six months, time needed before America could come to the rescue.

But these were old pre-war evaluations made forty years ago in 1902 when naval might was pre-eminent and air capability as a military tool was still in its infancy.[3]

With the imaginary protective gates closed, the men of the American and Philippine armies consolidated and set up defensive positions at Bataan peninsula to delay the advancing Japanese army.

---

[3] ibid

Why Japan Attacked: A Historical Perspective

For two hundred years dating back to 1600, Japan was isolated from the rest of the world by its own volition allowing few foreigners to step inside its borders. They were ruled by an Emperor who was a figurehead. *De facto* authority rested in a Shogun, an influential figure who held sway over the *deimyos*, feudal lords with an army. He made the hard decisions as to what was good for Japan.

The feudal lords were much like governors in states or provinces of today, with the exception that they held their position indefinitely. Beneath them to enforce the edicts of the Shogun were the soldiers, or *samurai,* who swore unbounded loyalty, even if it meant sacrificing their lives. On a mere whim, a *samurai* would gladly commit *seppuku*, a form of honorable death by self-stabbing if ordered by his lord.

In the 1800s, two Western nations, the British and the Dutch, were lucky enough to enter Japan on a limited trade basis. These countries at that time plied the seas of Southeast Asia and established colonies that provided the supply of tin, rubber, and other natural resources obtained from Malaysia, Singapore, Burma, Thailand, and parts of what is now the country of Indonesia.

Fifty years later, around 1845, the United States annexed the State of California to the Union, enabling the US to join other European players in the Asia trade in the Pacific. The steamboat fired by coal had just replaced the slow-moving sailing ships.

American ships began prowling the far reaches of Pacific Ocean in the hunt for whales, a then profitable industry as a source of oil. Oftentimes, by the time the ships' holds were filled to capacity with blubber, the coal bins were almost empty. They needed to obtain coal to fire the engines to make the return trip home.

Unpredictable typhoons in this area of the globe, a trademark of the wet monsoons, wrought an unintended consequence in the form of shipwrecks. American sailors perished. Those who survived got stranded on foreign shores and could not be rescued for many months or even years.

One country in particular where it was not a good place for a shipwrecked sailor to get stranded was the coast of Japan, where the survivors were harshly mistreated and denied any form of assistance.

As America thrived by becoming more industrialized, it was constantly in search of a source of coal, iron, and other raw materials to quench the thirsty bellies of its factories. Arriving in the Far East, America established trade relations with China and its neighboring country, Korea.

Along the route to these countries, the United States could not ignore Japan which lay in its path. There were intriguing reports of a mother lode of coal and iron in its bosom, so why not try to get in the good graces of the Japanese?

The Japanese shogunate was adamant, save for the lucky British and Dutch traders who somehow managed early on to get a foothold — no other foreigners were allowed.

Enter Commodore Matthew Perry, United States Navy. Following direct orders from the American president, Perry sailed boldly into Edo Harbor, now Tokyo Bay, with a wooden frigate and a squadron of four steam-engine-operated warships, an unheard of technology in Japan in those days. Next to the small, frail wooden Japanese sampans powered by sails and oars, one might think this would be enough to intimidate the local Japanese powers-that-be.

Perry sent a crew ashore with a letter from the American president, Millard Fillmore, to the local authorities at the harbor with a request that the letter be delivered to the Japanese Emperor.

The letter iterated America's wish to establish friendly relations with the Japanese. Perry presented a package of gifts for the Emperor, offering a tempting glimpse as to what lay in the world beyond the shores of Japan: a facsimile of a locomotive engine, a telegraph, an assortment of fine wines, and perfumes.

In reality, the Japanese Emperor was not the person in authority to make such a decision. He forwarded the letter posthaste to the Shogun, a process that took a relay of royal messengers on horseback several days of travel into the Japanese interior to the Shogun's residence.

The Shogun demurred. Who are these brazen foreigners? Opening the gate to America was a weighty decision that did not merit merely a casual discussion. After waiting a few days without a response to the letter to report back to the President, the American squadron discretely left the harbor.

President Fillmore waited a couple of years before re-ordering Commodore Perry to sail back to Japan. This time Perry set out with a larger squadron of warships. He now firmly requested a final answer to the US president's letter delivered previously. Looking at the imposing show of military might of America anchored menacingly in the bay, the Shogun flinched. He softened his stance and said yes.

The Japanese are a resilient people. Once the decision had been made to open their ports and their minds, they embraced the concept of industrialization. Japan thrived. Feeding on the diligence of its people, the country's production of goods started to exceed its supplies of raw materials. Japan also became an active player with the rest of the world. Although trading with America at the onset as a reward for opening its ports to the outside world, its hunger for raw materials increased. The Japanese beast demanded more supplies to stoke the red hot furnaces of its bustling factories.

The United States, Great Britain, and the Netherlands did not like competing in the Far East with Japan. They became like dogs quarrelling over the same bone. As a consequence, the western counties refused to share their resources gained from their Asian colonies with Japan. The United States tried to use this as a bargaining chip. The US would continue trade with Japan in exchange for certain concessions.

So Japan, now the hungry dog, went after its neighbors: China and Korea. Japan badgered China, who declined the former's overtures in regard to sharing their lodes of iron and coal. The push became a violent shove, leading to a series of escalating skirmishes between the two countries.

To its discredit, the once mighty Overlord of Asia, the celestial empire of China, did not keep up with the advancing trend of the Industrial Age. China became a pushover for the rancorous and modernized Japanese military that wielded the wand of military influence over them.

The tenuous relationship between China and belligerent Japan came to a head over a minor incident in remote Manchuria.

A Japanese private had gone AWOL after having crossed the Marco Polo Bridge, named in honor of the adventurous Italian merchant who traveled in this part of the world along the Silk Route years back.

The bridge, as it is today, was the point of entry into the city of Chinese Manchuria. The Japanese were denied permission by the Chinese guards to cross into the walled fortress in Mongolia to search for the missing Japanese soldier. After some harsh but fruitless verbal exchanges at the bridge, the Japanese withdrew.

Hours later, the angry Japanese came back in force, over-whelming the Chinese soldiers guarding the bridge, and attacking the fortress at Manchuria, despite the fact that the missing Japanese soldier had already returned to his unit.

The bottled-up enmity never fizzled; skirmishes became widespread over the following months and years. The Japanese continued the pressure pursuing the Chinese seat of government, which kept withdrawing deeper into the interior. But China is a vast land.

Japan became a victim of the same circumstances that Germany experienced when its forces invaded Russian soil and were caught in the quagmire of winter. Japan could not deliver a telling blow against China. Japan's military resources became stretched as it chased after the elusive Chinese seat of government.

Pressure against the Japanese by this time came from another front. America cut off its trade relations. In addition, all Japanese assets and money in the US were confiscated.

The United States rationalized that Japan manufactured bullets and munitions, from the ore and oil that America supplied, to kill Chinese who were US allies and trade partners.

Japan was left holding an empty bag. Job losses, depletion of food supply, a sagging economy, and graft and corruption among the Japanese politicians fomented heated discussions for a solution to the growing problem. Two factions emerged: the hawks who clamored vociferously for violent action and the doves in the minority, who wanted to accept the status quo and remain passive.

The hawks prevailed. Headed by Prime Minister Hideki Tojo, erstwhile general in the Japanese army and believer in ruthless militarism, formulated a plan: (1) seize control of Southeast Asia for its tin, rubber, and natural resources from the Dutch, French and British colonials who did not belong there to start with, (2) eradicate the Pacific Naval Fleet of America.

Pearl Harbor must be attacked and the American fleet eliminated. Then the Philippines and the rest of the Far East countries would become part of the Japanese empire.

Among the more rational hawks in the Japanese military, was one cause for concern with this line of aggressive thinking. Japan would win in the first round of a ten-round bloody fistfight, but America would win the final round. The reason—it had vast resources, while Japan did not— unless it could control the entire Far East.

History would prove the latter to be correct.

The First Meeting
1931

A trailing plume of white dust caught up to the old bus as it lurched to a halt in the center of town. The bus applied a generous coat of powder through the open windows to the passengers.

Tay, a thin young man in his early twenties, in a threadbare suit and shoes worn out at the soles, alighted. In his right hand he clasped a straw valise, its contents and everything else on his person constituting the sum total of his worldly belongings.

It had been a slow journey from his home almost seventy kilometers away. Today, the trip would take an hour over the rough, unpaved roads. The long wait for the old rickety bus took the greater part of the day to get to Bisal.

Because it was the only means of conveyance available, the driver had no qualms about loading as many passengers as he could as long as no one complained.

One old woman with three large pieces of baggage was allowed aboard. Helpful passengers strapped her load atop the bus. Nobody was turned down.

A man flagged down the bus. He had two large live pigs to be taken to market, but they were still roaming free in the fenced yard. Could the driver help? No problem. In fact, two other male passengers lent a hand.

Together, they corralled and trussed the hapless, squealing animals, finally hoisting them atop the roof of the bus, firmly nestled between a sack of rice and a basket of cackling chickens.

It was already mid-afternoon when Tay arrived in Bisal. He was a stranger, a newly minted schoolteacher, informed by a letter that appointed him to his first assignment. To slake his thirst, he headed for a free-flowing artesian well on the side of the road.

As he straightened from a quaff of the sweet cold water, he saw the school building over the fence, its name boldly printed on a sign beneath the overhanging roof. He was in the right place.

Two men came on horseback from the opposite direction, where a dike could be seen in the distance. They reined in by the well, sweat drenched the back of their shirts, dirt lined the furrows of skin across their foreheads.

The older man immediately jumped off his horse, one hand held the reins, the other grabbed the second horse's bridle.

The younger man touched a finger to his forehead in a cavalier salute at Tay before he dismounted. He regarded this stranger.

Tay smiled back, showing a slight gap between his front teeth. A large raisin-sized brown mole stood out over his right eyebrow.

An introductory conversation established that Tay was in town to teach at the school and that he had no place to stay.

Toribio, the young man, was about the same age as Tay. He had a light complexion, suggesting he was a *mestizo,* an offspring of a native and a Spaniard. He wore a longsleeved shirt open at the throat; a loose bandana hung around his neck. Despite the hot weather, he wore a *chalico,* a short vest Tay had seen worn by cowboys in a western movie.

The older man, Bolol, was his vassal. He spoke little and remained deferential to Toribio. Both men were in town on an errand to stack up on provisions at Teriong's store.

Toribio and Tay appeared to have similar interests, based on their conversation which morphed from horses, to guns, to cockfighting.

On this last subject, conversation became animated on the merits of the high jumping but smaller framed game cock to the more muscled likewise feisty game cock of another breed.

Bolol sighed and resignedly took both horses with him to finish the business they came to town to do. When his master, whom he addressed as *Patron*, was this engrossed, it was his duty to take the initiative. He came back an hour later with packs of merchandise secured behind the saddles on the rumps of the horses.

Tay and Toribio sat comfortably beneath the shade of an acacia tree addressing another pressing problem about mankind and the world in general,.

Realizing the time of the day, Toribio changed the subject and asked Tay where he was going to stay. Tay looked in the direction of the schoolhouse, silently inferring that he planned to sleep inside one of the classrooms.

Toribio would have none of it. Filipino hospitality has an unwritten rule: one offers food and shelter to any stranger in need. Toribio and Tay mounted the horses. Bolol remained behind to be picked up later by one of the servants. Toribio noted how easily Tay handled his horse and deduced that this man was not an equine novice.

Toribio's hacienda lay a few kilometers outside of town. They had to cross a creek. Toribio stretched his hand outlining the boundaries of his landholdings from that point on, as far as the eye could see.

Tay gazed in awe. A man who owned this much, whose father was not a native of the land in the strict sense of the word, must belong to a family powerful from the Spanish colonization of the country. They then entitled themselves as they cowed the previous owners of these lands into submission, seized their properties, and held the inhabitants under their control as vassals.

That no longer mattered. It was in the distant past. What happened long ago was not his business. He was sent here to teach.

The household, which included Toribio's wife and two boys, came out to greet him. Several of many servants came to tend the horses, unload the packs, and carry Tay's paltry suitcase up to his bedroom.

At dinner, plied by the effects of *basi,* the home-brewed fermented sugar wine, the two men continued their discussion well into the night.

6-Laki Pastor, Tay's father
He taught Tay how to shoot a rifle and ride bareback..

Tay explained that his skills at horseback riding, bareback at that, started on the hills of the land owned by his father, Pastor, where they raised goats and a few cattle. Armed with a pea shooter, he learned to ward off attacks by feral dogs that threatened to harm the livestock.

Noticing that he had become good at shooting small game, Pastor loaned him his own rifle and taught him how to use it. There was no telling when he might need to use it someday against roving bands of marauding robbers.

Tay stayed as a houseguest at Toribio's place for about six months. Then he got married.

Cupid's Arrow

Tay's status as a bachelor came to an abrupt end on his third month in Bisal. A petite, comely woman arrived at the school to teach. She was twenty-two and unattached. From the moment of their first encounter, Tay was stricken.

7-Nay, Felix's mother, November 21, 1932

Eros, in a moment of mischievousness, meant to fire a small arrow laced at its tip with a mere droplet of the love potion, but had grossly miscalculated on the potency of the dose.

Tay, the victim, clutched at his wounded breast and dropped to his knees, beyond help.

He was in love.

Toribio's wife, Carmen noticed that Tay had lost his appetite and became inattentive at mealtime conversations. Previously, he ate three square meals, but now he was wont to pick and not even eat dessert.

She also noticed that Tay was more fastidious about his appearance. He spent more time in front of the mirror before leaving the house, making sure every strand of his dark, wavy hair, heavily glossed with pomade, was impeccably combed and parted in the middle in the prevailing style of the time.

One day at school dismissal, as Nay was closing the door to her classroom, who happened to be leaving the classroom two doors away and was about to step out in the faint drizzle?

Heavens, it was Tay! One thing led to another, and before you could say CUPID, they were both sharing the shelter of Nay's itty-bitty umbrella. And it was hardly raining.

A scandal!

Rumors about the pair were fueled by other sightings, one being an inadvertent touching of their fingertips as Tay gallantly escorted her out to unlatch the closed gate of the schoolyard. More happened too frequently to be merely coincidental.

The conclusion was ominous. A courtship was abloom.

In the end, Tay proposed to Nay who initially demurred. She made him wait a few weeks, which caused a daily pang of anguish to Tay's tormented heart.

Finally, she answered, "Yes."

Next, there were a series of hoops to jump through. Nay chose a quiet time at dinner to gently inform her parents of an impending visit from Tay's father, Pastor, a widower.

Nay's parents, Cito and Juana, were not exactly unaware. News traveled fast in a town where everybody knew each other.

In anticipation of the visit, Cito ordered one of the free-roaming chickens to be caged and fattened for the upcoming dinner in honor of the guests and directed his wife to select his best *barong tagalog* shirt to be checked for tears, then ironed.

Finally, he checked the pantry and made sure the jug of home-brewed fermented wine, *basi*, was full.

On his part, Tay informed his father that he had found the woman of his dreams, and asked for his blessing.

Pastor sought the services of Adan, the local matchmaker from his hometown.

On a bright Saturday afternoon, Pastor, Tay, and Adan, all dressed in their Sunday best, trooped to the home of Nay's parents and hailed from outside the gate for permission to enter.

Nay's parents, likewise formally dressed, were inside the house. Although expecting this particular visit, Cito, Nay's father opened a window, and in a loud voice inquired perfunctorily who they were before allowing them to enter the premises and ascend the stairs.

The principals all sat in the living room, Nay's parents on one side, Tay, Pastor, and Adan on the other. Nay, who, by tradition remained out of sight, listened to the conversations from behind a curtained door to her bedroom. Adan, known for his flowery expressions and bombastic voice talked about mundane things.

"There is a beautiful flower in this house, whose fragrance is so sweet and irresistible that it has drawn the attention of a bee," the latter an oblique reference to Tay. For more than an hour he wove a net of hyperboles and metaphors and long-winded mention of subjects relevant or irrelevant to the purpose of the visit at hand.

61

Adan came to a long pause. He glanced in Cito's direction in hopes of an offer for a libation to wet his raspy throat.

Finding none, he concluded with the question, nay, a plea.

"Would the keeper of the flower be agreeable to a union of the flower with the bee?"

At a signal, the maid in the kitchen, who was eavesdropping behind the slightly open door, came out with glasses and a large wine jug. Upon hearing Cito's response in the affirmative, a toast with a glass of *basi* was proposed.

A round of wine followed a few more refills until the large jug was empty. Now it was Cito's turn to give his long narrative of a slurred acceptance speech agreeing to give Nay's hand in marriage, but it paled in comparison to the indomitable erudition of the well-practiced Adan.

By late afternoon following an early dinner, mission accomplished, they said their goodbyes and made ready to leave. Adan rose from his seat and swayed. Pastor alertly grabbed him by one arm, while Tay held him steady on the other. The three gentlemen tried not to embarrass themselves by not stumbling down the staircase on their way out.

8-Nay, Felix's mother, front, 1st on left
She taught in several school districts.

9-Nay, Felix's mother, seated front
Tay, father, 2nd from right back.
With fellow teachers during time of courting.

10-Tay, Felix's father, seated in 2nd row 4th from left
Note students who went to school with bare feet

Homestead

Not to be outdone, Don Toribio secured several hectares of vacant government land and claimed it as a homestead in behalf of Nay and Tay.

It had a pond in the back abutting a dike that ran for several kilometers, which dammed the river from flooding the central plain of the island in the monsoon season.

In anticipation of the wedding two months away, Don Toribio's vassals cut down bamboo trees and made nipa shingles from leaves of palm trees at the hacienda to cover the roof and walls.

When all necessary materials were ready, they set a date to build the house.

Over a weekend, his men and their families came with building materials, pots, pans, and food. Bolol took charge. They cleared a chosen spot, raised the ground with shoveled earth, and built a bamboo and nipa house without nails. It was erected on stilts, a necessary precaution for people who inhabit the central plain of Luzon, where flooding is a common annual happening during the monsoon season

In anticipation of a large family, Toribio made sure it had at least three bedrooms and a wide covered balcony at the top of the stairs to be used as a living room and to entertain guests. In the back of the house was an ample dining room and kitchen. Next came a *batalan,* a raised open porch at the back of the house, where a hand-operated water pump drew water ten feet from the level of the ground below. Here all laundry was done by hand on a large flat tub, the *batya*. An enclosed room served as the shower area. An outhouse was built about fifty yards away in the back.

The children of the families from Toribio's farm were sent to gather firewood, harvest snails, and pick fruit while the women cooked. It was a working festival enjoyed by all.

With so many willing and able hands joined in the task, the house was ready and finished by the second weekend.

The Goathole

Don Toribio and Tay developed an enduring friendship over the years. Their families spent much time together.

In Tay's yard, they grew a vegetable garden, raised pigs and chickens kept in coops at night and a small herd of goats. The goats were trained to come home to their pen every evening. In the morning, the nursing female goats were detained and milked for the family's consumption before their release to roam and graze freely on the verdant slopes of the nearby earthen dike.

One evening, the count was short one goat. Everyone fanned out in search beyond the hills without any luck. When darkness arrived, they trudged home prepared to resume the search the next day.

They heard the incessant familiar bark of their lead dog, Betty, above that of the other dogs. When they reached the backyard, they found all the dogs in a circle around a patch overgrown by *ipil* shrubs, a plant-food favorite loved by the goats for their luxuriant leaves.

Tay commanded the dogs to stop barking. In the ensuing silence, they heard muffled bleating. It was coming from a dark hole that no one knew existed. The missing goat had fallen in and was resting on a rock ledge below, it horns entangled on an overhanging branch.

On one social occasion at Tay's home in which Toribio and his family were present, Tay told him the story of the missing goat and walked him to the spot. It was henceforth known as the Goathole, a spot that the children were to avoid.

The Role of the Bisal Soldiers at Bataan

On January 6, 1942, Captain Toribio's company became assimilated by the Filipino and American forces under the command of an American general.

They were given an order to defend a small swath of land on the northeast corner inland of Bataan, where the peninsula became mountainous and the jungle at the foot of the mountain began.

The foliage of vines and trees hid dips between cliffs of rugged terrain inhabited by monkeys, snakes, and birds. It was impossible to cover such gaps between friendly units who were left with no choice but to get strung in a broken line.

Toribio's keen eye as a hunter perceived the difficulties in establishing a defensive perimeter, and he was worried.

He ordered Gonzalo, his master sergeant, to assign his best men at the company's flanks and to be especially vigilant at night.

On January 9, the vanguard of the Japanese army was finally in place. They began their first probing attacks on the eastern flank of the Bataan line in search of a vulnerable point. The Japanese met considerable resistance at first and even experienced a counterattack, which did not please their commander. He ordered patrols to reconnoiter around the perimeter northeast for chinks in the defensive lines.

Two weeks into the battle at Bataan, Captain Toribio's hunch was proven correct. His company's right flank was probed in the dead of night. The men could hear the occasional snap of broken twigs trampled on by unseen boots and the scree of loose rocks sliding off the mountainous slopes in front of them that led up to Toribio's men waiting in the trenches.

The captain decided to investigate. He slithered down the line behind the foxholes of his hunkered down men, and advised them to hold their fire and await his signal.

When he came to a low tree that signaled the end of the company line, he held his breath, waiting. He detected a faint shuffle of feet close to his position.

He pulled a flare gun from his belt and fired skyward.

Screams of *Banzai* pierced the night, and counters of alarm in the Filipino dialect triggered a torrent of gunfire from both sides.

Almost a hundred enemy soldiers, exposed in the glare of the bright light, their battle uniforms and helmets covered with twigs and leaves for camouflage, leaped forward on the open ground toward the flashes and the sound of gunfire.

Toribio dove headlong into the nearest available trench. Two soldiers in the foxhole fired at will at the enemy that knew only one direction: forward. And they were getting closer.

Exhorted by their officers behind them, the Japanese clambered over the fallen bodies of their comrades in wave after wave of frenzied attacks in an attempt to break down the defense by their sheer superiority in numbers.

By happenstance, both of Toribio's men in the trench had to reload at the same time, their rifles empty. Toribio stood up, exposing head and chest, firing over the heads of his men until he heard the despairing click of his own weapon.

Sensing an opportunity, a Japanese soldier rose from cover and ran directly at Toribio, fixed bayonet aimed at his face. Toribio dove sideways and blinked. He heard the impact of metal on metal followed by a dull thud like a shovel striking earth. Then, a grunt.

Toribio was unharmed. He had sought cover in a foxhole with Sergeant Gonzalo's and one of his men. While one hand groped for a fresh magazine to reload his rifle, Gonzalo looked up to see the point of a bayonet aimed in his direction. Reflexively, he reached for his native *bolo,* which lay sheathed at his belt, and made a wide overhead swat as if he were cutting *cogon* grass.

The blade of the bolo, sharp as a razor, struck the trigger guard of the Japanese soldier's weapon, glanced past the butt of the rifle, and slashed the soft unprotected belly of the enemy who came down with a deep final exhalation and was still.

The ubiquitous implement of the Filipino farmer, the *bolo,* had saved their lives.

The night attack was over in a matter of minutes, lasting only as long as it took for the flare to snuff itself out. Captain Toribio's line held, but he hardly paused for rest. He asked for a quick head count and shored up the defensive line.

At daybreak, he called his platoon commanders to a meeting. He was saddened to hear of the loss of one of his lieutenants, who was now replaced by Sergeant Gonzalo.

Upon entering the meeting area, Gonzalo was crestfallen.

"Capitan, my Patron," he gasped. "You are injured!" Gonzalo was unable to separate his personal relationship with Toribio from that of a soldier. In actual life, he was the son of Bolol, Toribio's main vassal at the *hacienda.*

Blood caked the seat of the captain's pants and the back of his legs. He had a tear over his back pocket where he had sustained a stab wound.

At that moment, he ignored it. He had more pressing matters to deal with.

The war in the Philippines was unfair as are all wars. In the desire to win, men feel an unending search for the ultimate weapon by either side bent on giving one an advantage in killing another human being. At Bataan and Corregidor, soldiers on the ground with their puny rifles could not defend themselves against artillery barrages and air bombings. Finding protective cover from the deadly missile addressed "to whom it may concern" required an extraordinary stroke of luck.

Men grumbled, some wishing the shelling would cease so that the real confrontation could begin, each stepping forth to fight the adversary man to man on more or less even terms. The withering cannon barrages went on, occasionally pausing, followed by a frontal jab by the enemy with infantry attacks in an attempt to gain ground.

Bayani

In the lull between barrages of cannon shelling, a lone Filipino soldier crawled through the battered landscape. Assigned to battalion headquarters, he had been sent to deliver a message in person to the company commander two hundred yards away, since the telephone lines were disrupted, a common problem throughout the war.

This was now the company's fourth defensive position, having received orders to withdraw yet again in the shrinking pocket of resistance against the advancing Japanese who outnumbered and outgunned them.

The messenger crawled past an abandoned howitzer looking intact but apparently useless, its incessant firing having melted the barrel. A dead water buffalo used to move the cannon to a different location lay close by, its carcass bloated. Empty and still unused artillery shells lay in a jumble of disarray like randomly thrown matchsticks.

He ignored the smell of corrupting bodies along his route, as it paled in comparison to the hunger pains in his stomach and the craving for water and rest. Crawling past a dead body, he noticed an intact canteen and dismissed the thought of drinking from it out of respect for the fallen man.

It was March 1942. Rations of food on the battlefield per man had been cut to one-third; water was supplied twice a day. The endurance indicator was about to reach the redline.

When the war started, this man, Bayani, was lean and fit, a second-year cadet at the Philippine Military Academy. A sense of pride welled in his chest as he recalled the last full-dress march when the entire regimental Corps of Cadets, resplendent in their shiny brass buttoned-tunics, white ducks, and ceremonial feathered headgear, marched for a mile in disciplined close formation and measured half strides, rifles at shoulder arms, ignoring the freezing rain on their way to the parade ground.

Finally facing the covered grandstand, the Corps commanding officer addressed the cadets over the loudspeaker with an urgent message that had arrived early in the day.

He announced, "War with Japan has been declared. By Presidential Proclamation all upperclassmen will be considered to have graduated and given military commissions with assignments to combat units of the Philippine army. Lower classmen were given the option of returning to their homes or joining the military as enlisted men."

A growing murmur spread throughout the entire regiment at this unexpected turn of events. The cadets could not absorb the magnitude of the orders given. Finally they had the chance to go to battle, a fierce ambition that had been in the backs of their minds since choosing to enter the hallowed halls of the academy.

To a majority of the cadets, there was no doubt. They would answer the call to duty in defense of their country. One of the lower-class cadets later formed a group called the Hunters ROTC—several hundred younger students. During the Japanese occupation, these students were actively involved in intelligence gathering and engaged the enemy on isolated Japanese outposts and patrols. The group attacked a Japanese armory, where several hundred rifles were taken. An American guerilla outfit worked with them, carrying out anti-Japanese activities. Filipino collaborators working with the Japanese were ferreted out by this group and killed. The Japanese offered a bounty for the capture of its leader.

Young Bayani, my uncle, twenty years old at the time and a second-year cadet at PMA, chose to join and fight as a private in the Philippine army assigned in Bataan.

Captain Toribio was at his command post, if one could call it that, a hole in the ground covered by a torn tarpaulin with a slate of rock for a table. He was startled to spot a soldier slithering into his location from out of nowhere in the dark.

Toribio's eyes widened at the sight of the soldier who saluted him. "Sorry to drop in so suddenly without warning, sir. Our telephone lines are not working. I have a message from battalion HQ." He stated the purpose of his visit

Bayani had prominent cheekbones, a toothy grin, and a piercing stare. He could have passed for Tay, my father, save for the fact that this man was four inches taller and did not have the raisin-sized mole over his right eyebrow that Tay was born with.

"I mistook you for someone I know." Toribio explained his friendship with Tay.

"He is my cousin, sir. We grew up together," Bayani recalled fondly. "His father, Pastor, and my father, Atong, are brothers."

For a brief respite from the war, he silently recalled the fun times in the summer, growing up tending cattle and goats in the large communal property of the clan up in the hills. Tay and Bayani rode the horse owned by Pastor in tandem bareback to herd the flock or hunt for rabbit and wild birds.

Breaking out of his reverie, Bayani saluted and made haste to go. Midway through his run in the broken terrain, he heard the familiar whistle of incoming shellfire.

Fueled by the increased thumping of his beating heart, his legs took on freshened vigor. He darted nervously like a cornered rabbit seeking cover, found a fresh crater, and dove in. He heard the whoomph, then saw the tumultuous upheaval of dug up earth, pieces of shrapnel over and around him. Bayani and the impacting cannon

74

shell seemed to have converged at the same spot. It was the last thing he could remember.

The countless hours of sleep deprivation and the lack of adequate food and water had already starved his brain cells. The concussion he suffered from the exploding shell was the final switch that rendered his bodily systems to go into hibernation mode.

He lay semi-comatose for almost a day. An ant tried to crawl inside his ear and woke him up with a start. Amazingly, he felt refreshed.

Looking about him, Bayani realized he was three feet from the point of impact of the cannon shell burst. The lip of the hole he had fallen into had shielded his face from the falling debris; a blanket of earth about half a foot deep covered his chest and lower body and legs; his rifle lay at an angle, the butt leaning against his right hip. His right ear went deaf; he heard a constant ringing within. Still, he marveled at his extreme good fortune.

He shrugged off the dirt as a dog would shag water off its back, crawled out of the hole, and rose to return to his unit.

The familiar shriek of an incoming artillery shell about to land in front of him made him dive back into his old crater. A stitch of sharp explosions blanketed the area between him and his unit. He knew that the pattern of barrages would be walked along this area soon, making his hiding place highly vulnerable. He ran back, eyes darting ahead, and recognized the tattered camouflage of tarpaulin. He hurtled head-on, hitting a sharp-edged rock with his helmet into the surprised Captain Toribio's foxhole.

When the shelling momentarily stopped, the two men clapped each other on the shoulders, sending a healthy cloud of brown, dry dust flying. Their bloodshot eyes and worried expressions mirrored the internal stress they had been going through. The captain took out his half-empty canteen, drank from it, then passed it to Bayani, who took a long swig followed by an

Atabrine pill, a strong smelling pill given to the troops to prevent malaria from the ever-present mosquitos.

Bayani narrated what he had been through since their previous encounter. Toribio looked up at the sky and listened attentively.

"It sounds too eerily quiet. I would guess the Japs will start blasting away again pretty soon, because there is still a lot of daylight left and the enemy spotters are watching every move we make. Why don't you stay until it is prudent to return to your unit?"

Bayani concurred. He had made the almost fatal mistake of being out in the open in broad daylight. To pass the time, they conversed sporadically about home and family into the darkness of the night, when Bayani felt it was safe to return to his unit.

Surrender of Bataan

Bataan and Corregidor were the last bastions of defense for the beleaguered American and Philippine forces. Going into the fourth month of the war, they had finally run out of wiggle room.

The defenders of Bataan began to feel the constant pressure of physical and mental exhaustion, hunger, and war wounds. They suffered dwindling amounts of food, medical supplies, and ammunition. The ultimate blow came with disease and dysentery from lack of clean water and living amid the corrupting corpses of the unburied dead.

They had punted and delayed the Japanese advance, hoping for reinforcements and the promise of help from the United States, which never came.

The bombing of American assets at Pearl Harbor in addition to commitment in the war in Europe would delay the process of succor.

Were it a chess match, the battle in the Philippines had come to an inevitable checkmate.

The Japanese forces had the advantage of controlling the pace of the conflict. When ammunition or manpower were low, they could pause without consequences while they waited for supplies and reinforcements. They had an unopposed air force that bombed Bataan and Corregidor at will. American naval capability was hampered.

Bataan fell first. The American general made a decision to surrender his troops to avert further casualties. He hoped for humane treatment by their captors.

On April 22, 1942, 80,000 soldiers surrendered—12,000 Americans and 68,000 Filipinos—a ratio of one to six.

The Japanese military was disconcerted. They expected a fight to an honorable death as drummed into their culture by the code of military thinking of the time, the way of the *samurai*. In their eyes, capitulation lowered the status of the surrenderers to a lesser being, so they treated the captives as such with contempt and utter cruelty.

The prisoners of war streamed out of Bataan under the watchful eyes of Japanese soldiers on a tortuous northward journey of 70 kilometers for internment in makeshift prison camps. Along the way, 5000 men faltered.

When the order to surrender filtered down the ranks, only eighty-five men, barely able to fight, survived from the original three hundred in Captain Toribio's company. Most of them came from the town of Bisal. He knew everyone. They knew and respected him as their leader.

He felt the weight of responsibility on his shoulders, experiencing moments of self-doubt as to whether he had sent them to their deaths on orders he probably should not have given. Tears welled and wet the front of his dirty uniform.

He turned so that his men could not see his face. He touched the seat of his pants to dry the tears on his hands. He winced as his fingers brushed against a tender area over his right hip, where he had developed a festering wound.

He realized he was sick. He shook off any feeling of self-pity, tried to clear his mind, and began to think.

What were his options? Here he was in Bataan, surrounded on the west and east by the enemy. South of them was Manila, guarded at the bay's entrance by the island of Corregidor, once an indomitable fortress, but wouldn't be much longer. North of him lay the mountain. Beyond that and farther east was home. He dwelt on this for hours while he marched with his men.

He knew how to live off the mountain. Once he was in his home area, he had family and his vassals who would help him. Escape by this route was not going to be a cake walk. His chance of surviving was slim. On the other hand, marching with his fellow prisoners meant certain death for him with his bad hip and growing physical deterioration.

Toribio motioned to Sergeant Gonzalo and outlined his plan.

Barok

Young Barok, age twenty-five, the school janitor, survived the war in Bataan along with his foxhole buddy and childhood friend, Ador.

When the order to surrender reached the ears of the men on the battlefield, Barok and Ador were unsure what they should do. They remained burrowed in the deep foxhole awhile awaiting guidance from Captain Toribio. Should they go with the rest of what was left of the company, joining the line of prisoners of war who were surrendering? Or should they take their chances and sneak away in the opposite direction?

Their dilemma was solved by a passing officer from an adjoining company who chanced upon their hiding place. He said the order came from the top and that meant everyone. It should be obeyed! They joined the growing procession of surrenderers in twos and threes. At the gathering point, they were met by Japanese soldiers who prodded them with their bayonets and ordered them to lay down their weapons and empty the contents in their pockets before joining the growing column of POWs.

They followed an arduous route absent a foothold of level road, just irregular patches of disheveled earth from the shellings and the uneven farmers' soil of the rice paddies. It was an ordeal to the wounded with leg injuries and the weakened who did not anticipate their journey to the prison camps would be so trying. The line of march began in the town of Mariveles at the tip of Bataan peninsula where it is closest to Corregidor. Japanese officers, some on horseback, rode or walked up and down the line, identifiable by their sidearms of swords and pistols. Impatient with the logjam, they shot laggards to death with impunity. To conserve ammunition, they dismounted and made prisoners kneel with heads bowed forward before decapitating them with an overhead swing of their long swords.

Emboldened by the example set by their superior officers, the soldiers took it upon themselves as a license to shoot or stab to death those too slow to move or whomever they pleased.

Sixty-five miles later, the endpoint of the march at the town of San Fernando, the column of POWS was split into two groups; one went to a makeshift camp in Cabanatuan. The second group was herded into a train headed for a second internment camp at Capas, Tarlac.

The train ride in the hot summer temperature was hell. The boxcars were roofed with corrugated iron; the sides were vertical slats of wood without windows for ventilation. The wide hinged door was a solid wall of corrugated iron barred shut from the outside. Approximately a hundred men were forced inside, crammed wall to wall in a standing position like packed sardines. By the time all of the train was completely loaded, the inside temperature was as hot as a baking oven. When the doors opened at the final destination, men staggered out, their faces as red as boiled lobsters. Some were pulled out already dead from asphyxiation and overheating.

Barok staggered out of the dark maw of the hot caboose and was about to jump when he noticed his buddy was not by his side. Quickly, he shouldered his way against the wave of the exiting captives until he found the unconscious figure of Ador slumped close to the wall. Grabbing him by his arm and belt buckle, he pulled him up and cajoled him to stand. Half dragging him, they jumped off the train in the nick of time before a sentry started to search for any stragglers left inside.

The men were lined up in a column; they marched on foot once again. The final destination was nowhere in sight, still seven miles away. Ador was disoriented, flushed with fever and not able to stand on his own. When it was time to move, Barok had to carry his friend on his back. One mile later, Barok faltered under the load. He laid his unconscious passenger down against a large rock to rest. A Japanese sentry approached menacingly. A fellow prisoner moved to help. They linked arms, half dragging Ador between them for the final few miles to a barbed-wire enclosure. They sat on the ground amid a throng of several thousand surrenderers. Outside the already crammed facility, hundreds more were streaming in.

Several interminable hours later, a senior Japanese officer swaggered to a makeshift platform, and with hands on hips demanded silence. In heavily accented English, he broadcast an extemporaneous speech over the tinny speaker system. "You are no longer soldiers but subhumans, because you have dishonorably surrendered. Do not expect special treatment, America has disavowed you and has abandoned you. Anyone trying to escape will not survive."

An estimated one hundred prisoners died every day at Camp O'Donnell and Cabanatuan prisons.

The fall of Bataan caused whoops of *Banzai* among the victorious Japanese troops, but Commanding General Homma was not entirely pleased.

Corregidor had not surrendered sooner than expected, in fact, had remained defiant. Homma's timetable for the conquest of the Philippines had gone far behind schedule, and his superiors in Tokyo were dismayed. There was still a war to fight in other countries in the Far East. Already, some of the regiments held in reserve to help him finish the conquest of the Philippines were being diverted to fight elsewhere.

He was in a quandary. How could he expedite the process to victory?

History of Isla de Corregidor

Corregidor Island has a storied past. Literally translated, it means Island of Correctors, suggesting that at one time it might have served as a customs clearinghouse checking documents of ships before entering Manila harbor. It was also a naval base of sorts for Spanish warships in their effort to spread the Christian faith and extend trade in the East Indies.

A succession of invaders had attempted to plunder Manila for its vaunted riches. Before Magellan discovered the Philippines, the reigning local ruler, Rajah Matanda, had already built a palisade fort of coconut tree trunks on the south bank of the Pasig River. The Sultan of Brunei, under whom Rajah Matanda was a vassal, gave him bronze cannons for its defense.

When the Spanish conquerors arrived, Matanda's fort was taken down and replaced with stronger materials of brick and stone. It was named Fort Santiago in honor of the patron Saint of Spain.

Erected around the fort and city was a roughly triangular wall of stone and concrete eight feet thick and twenty feet high surrounded on the southeast, by a dug-in river moat. It was named Intramuros. The Spanish colonialists were its first inhabitants within those walls. Spanish naval ships kept watch over the bay from Corregidor Island to monitor any vessels coming into the bay until the fort and wall was completed.

During the time of Spanish colonization, a few countries tried to play a game of "King of the Mountain" in an attempt to topple Spain's hold by attacking Manila in force. In 1600 and 1847 the Dutch tried twice, but unsuccessfully. In 1762 a British naval squadron and British troops harassed merchant shipping from Corregidor and briefly occupied Manila in what was known as the Seven Years war against Spain. Two years later, after the end of that war, Manila was restored as a colony of Spain following a treaty settlement.

The most brazen attempt happened fifty-three years after Spanish rule. In 1574 a Chinese pirate named Limahong entered Manila Bay with a fleet of sixty-five *sampans* powered by oar and sail loaded with 2000 soldiers, 2000 sailors, and 1500 women. He dropped anchor in the vicinity of Corregidor with a hostile intent to test the mettle of these bearded foreigners. He sent an attack party of six hundred men ashore and demanded the surrender of Manila.

Unfortunately, a severe typhoon occurred. The pirates lost some boats, and two hundred pirates drowned before they even reached the shore. Limahong's lieutenant, a Japanese mercenary named Sioco, who commanded the assault group, pressed on and attacked anyway. A fierce battle ensued. The commander of the Spanish garrison, Martin de Goiti, was captured and killed. His ears and nose were cut off. Sioco pocketed the body parts as a trophies he planned to present to Limahong as proof of victory. They killed natives, cutting off fingers for their golden rings; they ripped off earlobes for pendants. The acts of barbarity openly displayed by Sioco and his men demoralized the leaderless Spanish soldiers who beat a hasty retreat for the safety of Fort Santiago. Sioco and his men took off in hot pursuit and laid siege on the fort. They set fire to the thick wooden door. The terrified soldiers inside awaited their fate with despair. Sioco was so confident of victory that he did not watch his back.

Back at the recently pillaged village, the natives looked among the dead and became incensed. Their erstwhile ruler, Rajah Lakandula, had been slain. His fingers were missing. His wounded wife witnessed the Rajah's fingers being cut off to remove the large gold rings that adorned each digit while he was alive. Sobs and wails tugged at the heartstrings of those present. One man spoke up against the violence they had observed, seconded by others. Outrage rose to fever pitch. The angry horde picked up weapons, whatever was at hand—bolos, bows and arrows, spears and long poles, and slingshots—and advanced in the direction of Sioco's men. Although their weapons were comparatively primitive compared to the pirates' pikes, arquebuses, and battle-axes, they exploited their superiority in numbers. The long spears and ten-foot-long bamboo poles used to steer the *bancas* in the water proved to be their most effective weapons. They held each pirate at bay beyond the reach of their shorter pikes. The enemy's arquebuses once fired allowed no time to reload and prime for the next shot, hence became useless. The Filipinos countered with their own projectiles—arrows and a hail of thrown stones. The pirates were pinned, outnumbered, surrounded, and eventually disorganized. The seawater lapping on the beach ran red with the blood from both sides.

Sioco realized the battle had been lost. Reluctantly, he retreated toward the waiting *sampans* with what was left of his men to rejoin the pirate fleet waiting in the bay.

Limahong

Who was this man? Born to poor parents in China, he was forced to leave home because there was not enough food to sustain the family. He lived by his wits and slept off the streets as a common thief. The will to survive was powerful, and he excelled. He organized a band of urchins like himself who stole what they could. He refined his trade by demanding a "tax" for protection against rival gangs from the merchants in his territory.

As he grew older, he heard of a large band of pirates who raided the coastal villages of China. Brashly, he entered the pirate's lair and presented himself and his group of juveniles to the pirate leader who was taken by his spunk and audacity. The leader spared Limahong's life and dared him to prove his worth. Limahong excelled in his new calling by his ruthlessness and charismatic presence. He rapidly rose from the ranks of the pirate hierarchy. When the head of the band of pirates died, young Limahong became the unchallenged successor.

Under his leadership, the pirate fleet grew to thousands of *sampans*. A thousand more men were added, along with women captured on coastal raids. Well-organized pillages along the Chinese coast increased at an alarming rate. The rash of atrocities eventually reached the ear of the Celestial Emperor of China, who, in a placatory message asked Limahong to cease his piratical activities, which fell on deaf ears. The coastline of China is infinite. He moved his fleet, randomly attacking in an unpredictable pattern. Pirate activity hardly abated. The Emperor, normally a peaceful monarch, acceded to pleas from his subjects for assistance. He ordered his war vessels to find and stop Limahong.

Limahong had no recourse but to flee from China. He roamed the high seas in search of bounty elsewhere. On one occasion, boarding a captured merchant vessel, his eyes widened at the prize in front of him—piles of dinner plates hammered out of gold, pearls the size of ostrich eggs, exquisite lace. He wanted more of the same. Limahong compelled the merchant captain to reverse course and lead him to this intriguing place, Filipinas.

A group of islands inhabited by friendly natives was discovered by Ferdinand Magellan fifty years before Limahong arrived. He claimed it as a colony of Spain. It was named in honor of its king, Phillip the Second. Thus, the name Filipinas. In the present day, the Philippines.

After several weeks of slow sailing southward from the China Sea, the pirate fleet sighted the northwest coast of Luzon Island, one of the largest islands in the Philippines, an area now called Ilocos province. It could not have come at a better time; the fleet was low on food provisions and fresh water.

Limahong sent men ashore, who got what they needed. But they could not resist leaving a trademark calling card they used in China. Before departing, they burned the huts of nipa and bamboo in the villages, petrifying their inhabitants.

What Limahong and his men did attracted the attention of Spanish commander Juan Salcedo and his army of soldiers who happened to be on official business close by.

Although he was only a young man in his late twenties, Salcedo wielded considerable military authority. Not only was he the nephew of the Governor General of the Philippines, Miguel Legaspi, he was also *de facto* enforcer of law and order throughout the Philippine colony. Salcedo collated the stories from the villagers, noted the size of the invading force, and surmised Limahong was after a bigger booty; the pirate fleet was bound for Manila and probably intended to sack it. Irked by the verve and pluck of this interloper of thieves and brigands, Salcedo assembled as many soldiers as he could and sailed posthaste for Manila.

It is easy to imagine Juan Salcedo's journey back to Manila, a distance of over two hundred miles that took many weeks to travel. One can conjecture that given the early lead of the pirate fleet, Salcedo's soldiers would probably not have been able to catch up in time to confront Limahong.

But Limahong was also traveling at a slow sailing pace dictated by the whim of tropical winds and ocean currents. He needed to stop often along the way for supplies to be able to feed his sizeable force. Salcedo guessed correctly. It took three months for Limahong and his pirates to finally arrive at the mouth of Manila Bay.

Limahong: The Second Seige

The defeated Sioco, simmering with anger, reported back to Limahong with what was left of his war party. Feeling humiliated, he cast the nose and ears of the fallen Spanish commander Martin de Goiti, the trophy he planned to present to Limahong were he to emerge victorious, overboard into the sea before groveling at Limahong's feet. Limahong stalked off to his cabin without saying a word in rebuke. Sioco was one of his best men. He remained in his room while he pondered his next move. Two days later, he emerged with a plan.

A second attack would be made with twice as many soldiers. His *sampans* would move closer to shore to provide cannon support, and he would give Sioco another chance to redeem himself by leading the attack. Unfortunately by this time, Juan Salcedo had already arrived with reinforcements and was waiting for the pirates with a solid battle plan. He stationed several hundred soldiers with arquebuses loaded at the fort's ramparts. At his command, a fusillade of bullets met the first wave of Sioco's men. While the front line of soldiers knelt to load and prime their rifles, another line of defenders came forth to lay a continuous cover of fire. Eighty men fell from Sioco's frontal attack. Taking advantage of the temporary disarray of the enemy he had anticipated, Salcedo ordered the Fort of Santiago's main gate opened. Hundreds of his men in armor breastplates, armed with shields, pikes, and battle-axes, poured out in a disciplined advancing phalanx. Bloody hand-to-hand fighting ensued. Neither side asked for quarter. Salcedo bided his time before seeking Sioco to bring the fight to an end. If the head of the snake is cut off, victory will be in favor of the defenders. Sioco was determined. He could not bear the ignominy of facing Limahong again if he did not win. A slash from his sword bloodied Salcedo's shoulder, but the latter, a schooled fencing master, stood firm. One of Salcedo's men, seeing his leader in distress, lunged at Sioco, who parried the blow. Salcedo had a clear shot at Sioco's unprotected neck. Sioco fell. The battle was over, and it was a decisive one.

Limahong pulled back his fleet on the bay to Corregidor but stubbornly refused to leave. Even in defeat, he intended to harass merchant vessels trying to enter Manila harbor. General Salcedo kept the pirate fleet at bay; he maintained a substantial land army that denied them points of access to a repeat invasion by sea.

Weeks later, Limahong, unable to land to procure fresh food and meat from local villages, cast off and sailed northward checking the coves as he hugged the Philippine coastline. He discovered the mouth of the Agno River, where it connected to Lingayen Gulf, the same body of water where General MacArthur was to land his liberating forces against the Japanese invaders in 1945, four hundred years later. Limahong convinced the natives that he had vanquished the Spaniards. He settled in and established a floating village in a nice harbor that teemed with fish!

News of Limahong's whereabouts eventually reached Salcedo's ears, who went after him again, traveling on foot and horseback with his soldiers. Along the way, he developed alliances with local *datus*. He tarried in their villages for a few days or weeks to allow for re-supply and rest for his men and horses. He was granted additional men for his growing army. In return, he promised material rewards from his benefactors, which the local Spanish friars and local clerks noted for the record.

Byproducts of these rest stops were the births one year later of *mestizos* and *mestizas*, fathered by the soldiers on their line of march.

The surprise raid by the Spaniards caught Limahong utterly by surprise; he was forced to withdraw from the Philippines for good.

Corregidor Island's strategic importance in defense of Manila Bay was no longer in question. The Spanish authorities assigned a permanent watch vessel and twenty men on the island to warn them of the approach of any suspicious ships entering the bay.

One of the contributors to Salcedo's army was Datu Masiken (meaning old), a wise and fair man who held sway and influence over what would be the equivalent to several towns today. This *datu* was the great ancestor of my paternal grandfather, Pastor.

The Spanish American War

Three hundred seventy-seven years later following Magellan's discovery of the Philippines, the Americans declared war against Spain on May 1, 1898. The antecedent reasoning which triggered the conflict is convoluted. It appears to be political and economic. It was historically precipitated by an explosion on board the USS Maine while it was anchored in Cuba, then a Spanish colony.

Commodore George Dewey, in command of the modernized American Naval Squadron stationed in Hong Kong, was given the order to attack the Philippine colony. He entered Manila Bay on board his flagship, the armored cruiser USS Olympia under Captain Gridley. At night without lights, the Olympia was undetected by the Spanish warships at Corregidor.

It was in this sea battle where Dewey uttered the infamous statement, "You may fire when ready, Mr. Gridley." The surprise attack quickly annihilated the antiquated wood flotilla of the Spanish Navy, wresting the Philippines from Spanish domination forever.

Under the terms of surrender following America's victory, the United States agreed to pay the then princely sum of twenty million dollars to Spain in return for cessation of the latter's territorial rights to the islands of Cuba, Puerto Rico, and the Philippines. America became the overseer of the Philippines and declared it a Commonwealth.

When its new owners looked at the map of the Philippines, they perceived the intriguing military potential of Isla de Corregidor in Manila Bay. This was at a time when a contentious relationship was developing with the ascending power in the Far East, Japan.

A blueprint for a defensive fort was drafted. From 1899 to 1903, America shipped the most advanced weaponry of that era, built from its own foundries. At Corregidor, they emplaced two long cannons with a range of seventeen miles. Hypothetically, they could cover the approaches of any enemy vessel entering Manila Bay. In actual combat during the war with Japan in 1941, these long cannons were ineffective: the barrels could not be depressed low enough, and the Japanese warships sailed in unharmed under the overshot cannon shells.

U.S. Troops on Corregidor

Isla de Corregidor's landscape was transformed into a garrison bristling with twenty-three batteries: 56 coastal guns, 13 anti-aircraft batteries, 76 anti-aircraft guns, 48 fifty caliber guns, and 10 sixty-inch Sperry searchlights.

Scattered around the bay, three other lesser islands, Fraile, Caballo, and Carabao were likewise fortified. Carabao Island lay only 500 yards from the Cavite coastline. It had 400 Philippine Scouts to man long 350 mm and 152 mm guns and anti-aircraft. Caballo Island, immediately south of Corregidor, had 800 marines and navy personnel armed with anti-aircraft and cannon.

Tiny Fraile island was roughly an acre in size, its flattened crown barely above the waterline. Reinforced concrete and steel were poured in to create a stationary "battleship" on which 200 men crewed battery emplacements, armored turrets, and secondary batteries. In theory, the Philippines should have been able to withstand a seaborne siege for six months until help arrived. At that time, 1901, army and naval strength were the only primordial weapons of war. Air power was still non-existent; note that the Wright brothers made their first airplane flight in 1903.

A symbolic memento of the victory from the Spanish-American war, the main mast of a vanquished Spanish warship was made into a flagpole and erected at the highest point of Corregidor.

From the air, Corregidor resembles a 1400-acre tadpole, four miles long and one and a half mile wide at its broadest. From a three dimensional view, it appeared like a four-legged animal sitting on its haunches rising four hundred feet at the head and about two hundred feet above sea level at its tail.

Paved roads and twenty miles of electric railroad tracks were laid to haul heavy equipment to the different batteries. A tram for passenger conveyance ran from 6 a.m. to 10 p.m. Counting all the stops, it was a thirty-minute ride from Topside, the widest and highest point, to the tadpole's tail, Bottomside.

A tunnel was dug two hundred feet beneath Malinta hill by prisoners to create a bombproof shelter close to the bottom of the island. The word Malinta derives from the local dialect meaning "full of leeches" because the surrounding swampy land was infested with these black, slimy, blood-sucking creatures. A double-track trolley cut through the middle of the vast tunnel shaped like a fish's spine with diagonal tunnels coming off the main track.

In an emergency, Malinta tunnel had room to accommodate a thousand casualties, not to mention the command center, personnel needed to maintain it, and supplies. In WWII, which ensued years later, it housed double that amount.

In the early 1900s, getting assigned to Corregidor meant a month of ship travel across the Pacific Ocean. It was an irresistible invitation for troops who could bring their families along as an incentive to see the other side of the world. Chance shipboard meetings with bachelor officers and daughters of other officers on these long trips sometimes developed into marriages.

Living on Corregidor was not like the recruiting posters on the walls of the local post offices—swaying coconut trees, lovely sunsets, tropical flowers, and blue sea. Termites and cockroaches infested the island, which taxed the ingenuity of its inhabitants. Mildew was not good for upholstery; glued furniture came apart due to the dampness. Because they dried quickly, rattan and wicker furniture, and straw and hemp mats became the preferred items for living in these conditions.

There was a silver lining. Military personnel who brought families were provided residential homes; they built the Mile Long Barracks for the bachelors and a hospital. A school was available for the American and Filipino children. There was a baseball field, a communal swimming pool, a theater, tennis courts, a golf course, churches, and bake shops.

A mine-laying vessel was converted with a secondary task. Twice a week, she plied the waters between Corregidor and Manila carrying passengers for a day of fun and nightclubbing in the vibrant city. An overhead awning on the top deck shielded the wives and officers from the glare of the hot sun while they sipped cocktails.

Tailor-made dress white jackets with monograms were provided by an entrepreneurial native who came periodically to make minor alterations as the girths of his customers expanded, fueled by good eating and fine spirits.

Housewives could hire Filipinos for cheap domestic help—a cook, housecleaner, babysitter, or laundry woman could be employed for the equivalent amount of seven dollars a month.

It was not uncommon for the officers living at Topside, on their way back from a weary day at the golf course or baseball field, to be asked to stop by someone's home for a drink, followed by, "Why don't you ask your wife to come over for dinner?"

The invitee would ring his wife on the party line, who in turn told her cook to prepare food for a potluck dinner to be taken to the hosting party's home. The preparations included plates, silverware, and maids and man-servants who provided waiter service.

High ranking officers' homes had the extra privilege of having a small swimming pool in the backyard, which they affectionately dubbed "carabao wallows," named after the muddy depressions in the fields where the water buffalos laid their bodies to cool. The swimming pools were ten-by-twelve-foot holes in the ground built with hollow blocks, concrete, and porcelain tiles.

The amiable commander of the island garrison decreed that in their free time, which was considerable since it was peacetime, the men were to choose a sport—baseball, golf, or both—to keep them in decent physical shape and to reduce increased visits to the post exchange for liquor and cigarettes. Two baseball teams were cobbled up, but although there was no shortage of players, it was curious that some of the men on both sides failed to finish the nine innings required. The team captain suspected that some of the players were bringing liquor in their bags and were using it to hydrate themselves in place of water in the tropical heat and humidity.

In a spirit of good-natured sportsmanship, the team captains capitulated and decided on a compromise—finish the rest of the innings the next day…if it was not raining. In the latter case, no one was excused from reporting to play, because it would be against the commander's rules. Instead, they would repair to the Officers' Club to finish the "meeting," which kept the bartenders busy.

One day on a trip to the local post office, Vince Kehaya, a cowboy from Montana, had spotted an alluring recruiting poster to "get a once in a lifetime chance to explore the other side of the world with its bucolic atmosphere and lithe brown maidens." At age eighteen and barely out of high school, he was bored of the rough and tumble life of a cowboy branding unwilling cattle and roping mean-spirited wild horses that tried to unseat him and even bite him given the chance. He decided to enlist.

Following weeks of going through the enlistment process and training as a Signal Corpsman, he found himself aboard a slow transport ship. One month later, he landed in the paradise island of his dreams on the shore of Corregidor. His duties were to receive and encode incoming and outgoing messages at Malinta tunnel dug beneath a hill. On occasion, his sergeant would send him on errands to hand deliver "eyes only" messages to ranking officers in their homes or at the golf course or baseball field.

Kehaya looked forward to such errands that allowed him to venture out, stretch his legs, and enjoy a smoke or two of his favorite Camel cigarettes, while soaking in the sunshine and balmy breeze. Some days, on his way back to his job, he veered off the path to find his way down a gap in the low cliff for a quick swim in the warm sea. At the sight of the baseball field, he adjusted his enlisted man's cap at a jaunty angle and checked the buttons of his uniform. Who knew what the marine commander might say about his appearance when he presented himself? He walked along the outfield fence toward a game in progress.

Crack! At the sound of the bat solidly hitting the baseball at its sweet spot, Kehaya looked to his right to see the gloved hand of the centerfielder extended in his direction. He glanced upward at the cloudless sky and realized the baseball was going well past the chain link fence. Instinctively, he tracked the ball as it sailed over his head, locked onto it, ran sideways to his left, and stuck out his bare hand. He felt the ball in his left palm and held it with a vise grip as if he were roping a steer in Montana.

Kehaya disappeared off the edge of a shallow cliff. Luck was with him. He got entangled precariously amid a thick bramble of wild poinsettia growing off a split in the rock. Beneath him, the frothing waves beat at the shore in a monotonous sequence, awaiting his landing in vain.

The concerned centerfielder vaulted over the fence and found Kehaya, ball nestled in his hand. By that time, the rest of the players had caught up to them, followed by the umpire who raised a closed fist and declared OUT!

Three men formed a line holding to each one for support. The last man extended his hand and extricated Kehaya to safety. The teams decided they'd had enough excitement for the day and repaired to the officers' bar, noncom Kehaya in tow. The conversation centered on the sensational overhead fly ball caught barehanded with Kehaya's non-dominant hand!

After reading the message delivered by Kehaya, the ranking officer asked him where he played ball. He replied, "Sir, I've never touched a baseball in my life. All I know is, when I used to rope steer for branding, my dad always told me to go for the horns and to never let go. The last time I didn't, and I almost got gored in the ass. Lesson learned."

The marine officer rapped at the bar with his brimming mug of beer for silence. "As senior officer, I am claiming Corpsman Kehaya to the Officers Baseball Team under Rule 13-1." It was a non-existent rule he made up exempting enlisted men from joining the OBT.

"From here on, he will be my team's centerfielder."

-o-

This life of bliss was not to last forever. In 1941, a few months before December, news of deteriorating relations with Japan came to the Americans.

The stark reality in a time of conflict—Corregidor was a military fortress and garrison. With the complement of gun batteries on the lesser islands around at Fraile, Caballo, and Carabao, the defense of Manila Bay was hypothetically solid, impregnable.

In the few months before the bombing of Pearl Harbor, a rumor circulated that war with Japan would be only a matter of time, even imminent. Quietly, women and children returned to America leaving the men to prepare for the serious business they had signed up to do: put their lives on the line to defend America's interests.

-o-

December 8, 1941/8:42 a.m.:

Signal Corpsman Vince Kehaya, earphones on by the switchboard, had just decoded an incoming message about the bombing of Pearl Harbor. He motioned frantically to the Master Sergeant on duty, Orville Powell, to verify. In turn, he ordered Vince, adding a few expletives, "This is hot! Get on the jeep and get this message in person right away to the Old Man."

This was a sensitive message for the commander's ears only, not for everyone who could listen in on the open party line.

Powell checked his watch. "You have three minutes to catch the 09:00 tram. I will alert the others in the chain of command."

Vince braked the jeep in a cloud of dust, leaving the key in the ignition. He was barely inside the tram before it started to move. It would be a long thirty-minute trip to Topside, then a one-minute sprint to the commander's quarters on Officers Lane.

Along the ascent from Bottomside, he could see the gun batteries guarded by a lone sentry, nothing frenetic at the moment. But the message inside his shirt pocket left no doubt that things would soon change.

And change it did. Four days later, after an amphibious landing in the northernmost shore of the Philippines, Japanese aircraft began probing the defenses of Corregidor.

The enemy dropped bombs on Middleside Barracks, where the enlisted marines were billeted, and the nearby hospital despite the prominently painted cross on its roof.

Malinta Tunnel became a medical facility, communications center, and headquarters for the highest ranked officers. Along the walls of the tunnels, stacks of supplies six feet high were unloaded from the trolley cars as fast as they could haul them in.

Soldiers who manned the big guns of Corregidor were kept busy day and night doing what it was built to do: protect the island and support the troops embedded at Bataan peninsula.

Bayani's Dilemma

Bayani was befuddled by the order to surrender Bataan to the Japanese army. Having been assigned away from the front at the command post, he had fired no more than a few shots at the enemy.

His most salient contribution thus far was as a messenger to front line units when normal lines of communication were disrupted. His warrior instinct goaded him to do more to fulfill what he perceived was his destiny.

His immediate superior understood Bayani's wish. Silently, he gave him his blessing by looking the other way while Bayani went in the opposite direction of the surrendering stream of his fellow soldiers and headed for the Bataan shoreline.

Bayani, on his passage through the community, came upon groups of Filipino families huddled in foxholes under their shade trees. Each hole was usually large enough for an entire family——father, mother, siblings, and grandparents—who slept on straw mats in the hole or on the ground nearby, ready to jump in when the shelling started. Soldiers also filled the families' yards, fighting the war from the vantage point of their own foxholes.

Civilians—old men, women, and children, all emaciated, dehydrated, dirty, hungry, and scared— had no place to go in the midst of the conflict. Their only possessions were the small parcels of land that lay beneath their feet.

An old woman pointed Bayani in the direction he wanted to go. Hours later, he saw a line of Filipino and American soldiers on the beach heading toward several barges, their engines idling.

A Marine captain waved him to a waiting barge and shouted, "On the double, soldier. We're leaving." The restraining boat ropes were released, and one barge after another laden with men took off on a heading for Corregidor two miles across the intervening water from the shore of Bataan.

The US Marine regiment in charge of the defense of the island assimilated the new arrivals: cooks, typists, navy officers and their men whose boats had been sunk, musicians in the marching band, sundry survivors from various infantry units of the US and Philippine armies.

The new arrivals swelled the ranks of the Marines already in place in Corregidor to the comforting total number of 4,000, more than enough men for a regiment. The soldiers were assigned to companies P, Q, and up, an unheard of amount of companies for one regiment. It left a good feeling, but it was misleading. Only a fourth were original Marines trained for ground combat.

Many were physically unfit to fight. By rights, a good number should have been in a hospital receiving medical treatment, but the thousand-bed capacity inside Malinta tunnel was already filled beyond its limits.

Moreover, the existing conditions inside the tunnel were less than optimal: the air was suffocating, stuffy and damp despite giant fans that vented the facility to the outside. When bombs dropped, dust and flying insects came in swarms from the ceiling like a fog. Bedbugs infested mattresses and cushions. The smell of sickness prevailed, which disinfectant could not mask. Even sick men preferred the open trenches and foxholes around the island.

Bayani became a squad leader of several soldiers, most of whom had not seen a weapon up close. One man—a musician in the marching band, who bore a permanent indentation on his upper lip from countless hours of playing the trumpet—looked askance at his rifle.

Bayani gave his squad of ten men crash instructions in caring for, loading, and firing their firearms. During lulls from incoming artillery, they sighted at floating debris on the water for target practice.

When Bataan fell, Japanese aircraft owned the air. They bombed and strafed the island at will. Day and night, artillery shells bombarded every inch of Corregidor from land positions gained along the southern shore of Bataan by the enemy. Although Corregidor still had the ability to respond with countershelling, General Wainwright expressed caution. He was unsure if there were POWs at Bataan who could become victims of friendly fire.

Postwar estimates show that the Japanese dropped fifty thousand tons of bombs on the first day alone in their drive to take Corregidor after Bataan fell, the most heavily bombed target in World War II next to the island of Malta.

Japanese spotters, fully aware that Americans no longer had air capability to shoot them out of the sky, were sent up in observation balloons from the Bataan shore. They could stay aloft as long as they wished. Any activity at Corregidor was reported to gunners manning cannons on the ground who pelted shells at spotted targets. This made it difficult to deliver food and water and tend to the wounded on the battlefield. Japanese airplanes dropped bombs— not once but twice or more times at the same target, just to be sure.

During short lulls in the bombardment, the carcasses of dead horses from the cavalry at the beleaguered island fortress were dragged into the underground mess kitchens and carved for meat. Water rations could no longer be brought in by ship from across the short span of two miles from the Mariveles water filtration plant. Fortunately, the US Marines had dug small freshwater wells in Corregidor before the war. They now scooped the precious liquid into empty cartons, milk bottles, and basins to deliver to the thirsty men.

This military strategy of saturation bombing, though painful if one were sympathetic to the defenders, makes sense. Why would the aggressor want to risk unnecessary casualties for his men if it could be avoided?

In the trenches, the men at Corregidor crouched for their lives, inhaling the constant swirl of brown dust that never settled and covered helmets and uniforms.

Every inch of uncovered skin, eyelashes, eyelids, and faces were coated with thick layers of brown masks and mascara from the omnipresent dust cloud as one bomb after another landed and stirred up the tortured earth. Only the whites of their eyes offered a contrast; the holes of their nostrils and mouths outlined the landmarks of a face.

The injured with open wounds suffered even more with the bacteria from the dust settling on the open sores as an unwanted scab in place of a sterile dressing.

Bayani was still a lucky man. His dirty uniform was torn from hugging the ground in his foxhole amidst countless flying shrapnel that littered the pockmarked ground around him.

He regarded the soldier who shared the foxhole next to him, cowering in fear, eyes unblinking, red blood vessels starkly outlined against the whites of his eyes like a man crazed by the incessant pressure.

Bayani shuddered at the spectacle of his fellow soldier, a shell of his former self. He felt afraid for himself in that he would give in to his own terror, then panic and turn tail. He looked away.

In so doing, he smelled the powerful reek of unwashed body: his own. He coughed deep from his chest and spat out brown muddy phlegm that had settled inside his breathing passages.

"I am rotting inside," he thought, like an actor saying his line as a comedic relief in a serious part of a play. He smiled at his witty remark. He felt himself about to let out a loud guffaw when he realized where he was. He giggled softly instead, burying his face between his folded arms.

In early April 1942, the night was cloudless with one solitary distant winking star. Soon there would be showers. The night had become eerily quiet. Did the enemy take a night off to charge their batteries?

A little past midnight, Bayani saw dark figures in the water. Nobody seemed alarmed. No one was firing at them. Realizing who they were, he stood, then slid down the forty-foot cliff and picked his way through a fissure of sloping ground. Holding the branch of a fallen tree, he found his way to the graveled floor below.

He broke off at a quick run in the direction of the intrepid group of his fellow soldiers who were bathing. His boots hit the smooth, level sand and he kept on running until he felt the splash of water. Still wearing his boots, clothes, and helmet, rifle across his back, he dove under the surface, relishing the warm tropical water as it washed the grime from his body.

When he came up for air, he heard the rhythmic pounding of the waves hitting the surf and saw the subdued glow of the frothing water in the darkness as if it were peacetime. He felt rejuvenated.

With his helmet he poured seawater over his head, ignoring the flotsam of broken boxes and planks of wood around him. He could smell the reek of floating diesel oil from the ruptured fuel tanks of the seven sunken Filipino maritime ships with their doomed crew that had been hit by enemy fire as they tried in vain to deliver food cargo to the starving troops at Corregidor. Fifteen minutes later he was back in his trench smelling like a diesel ship mechanic, but he didn't mind. It was his first bath in a long time.

It took a month after the fall of Bataan before the Japanese had the final cog in place to go on the offensive to overrun Corregidor.

Japanese General Homma, in overall charge, was losing his patience. So were his superiors in the military drawing boards in Tokyo. The Japanese offensive was running way behind schedule to take control of other countries in the Far East. Because of the recalcitrant defense of the American and Filipino forces, he constantly pressed his subordinate officer at Bataan for an answer.

What is the problem? We are behind schedule. Take Corregidor now!

At the risk of literally losing his head, the Japanese colonel tasked with leading the beach attack on Corregidor spoke in a low voice and explained the logistical problems causing the delay.

The undamaged landing barges needed to transport the troops for the invasion had to sail from the west at Subic Bay, then around the body of water between Bataan and Corregidor where boats were vulnerable to cannon fire from Corregidor before arrival at the final assembly point. Hence, the boats had to be moved in short legs of the journey and only at night so as not to telegraph their intent to the soldiers at Corregidor.

Also, an outbreak of malaria had afflicted the Japanese troops needed for the offensive. Time was needed to allow the sick to recover after being medicated with quinine. The colonel hinted to his commanding general that fresh reinforcements would be helpful.

11-Surrender of US and Filipino troops to Japanese.
In front of Malinta Tunnel, Corregidor, 1942.

---

4 Ullstein bild Dtl., Getty Images—https://www.gettyimages.com/

Japanese Attack on Corregidor: Final Offensive

Twenty-four hours before the Japanese Army launched the big offensive against Corregidor, 16,000 artillery shells rained on the garrison island. Then it was quiet.

The calm before the storm.

Bayani and the men assigned to a platoon of men at the north end of the Tadpole's tail facing Bataan took advantage of the lull to assess the perimeter defenses. Everything was in shambles from the bombings, with no time to make repairs. They prepared for the siege they knew was imminent.

At midnight, the droning sound of many engines grew louder across the dark water in the direction of Bataan, only two to three miles in front of them. The sound seemed to be headed toward the tail end of Corregidor. The Japanese boats were beset by the high tide and strong currents that had just changed. These confused the boat pilots in a directional sense, sending the boats crabbing sideways in an attempt to reach their assigned landing points. Searchlights turned from the shore of the defender revealed bobbing boats in helpless disarray. A hail of fire from several machine guns struck the first wave of Japanese barges. Their thin armor plating was easily penetrated by high-powered bullets that killed enemy soldiers hiding behind the steel walls. In an effort to escape the killing zone and save the barges, Japanese boat pilots ordered their soldiers to offload prematurely. They jumped into the water where it was still too deep. Laden with their rifles, backpacks, and extra loads of ammunition they were supposed to share with the other soldiers once ashore, many drowned. The carnage abated when the

Japanese shot out the searchlights. The persistence of the enemy landing force slowly paid off. A beachhead was finally established.

-o-

Bayani made the sign of the cross and thought of his family. It was time.

Along with the rest of the defenders of the tadpole's tail, Bayani stood in the deep trench next to a fifty-caliber machine gun team that began to fire tracer bullets. He hunkered close to the lip of his shelter, unable to fire. The enemy was still beyond the range of his rifle.

In the flashes of gunfire, he discerned the box-shaped outlines of the approaching enemy barges. He made himself useful by giving boxes of ammunition to the gunner's assistant, who continued to feed the hungry belly of his chattering machine gun. Strewn around his feet lay a growing mound of hundreds of discarded brass shells. The gun barrel glowed softly with heat in the dark.

The defenders of Corregidor kept the Japanese pinned down on the beach, but not for long, as more reinforcements arrived to make up for the casualties. Round two was about to begin and the outcome seemed, ominously, in favor of the Japanese.

At a shouted command, the Japanese dashed forward for the base of the low cliff to make room for the next wave of troops establishing a beachhead.

Banzai! The vanguard of the enemy troops, out of what was left uninjured of the first wave of the landing force, ran on the beach to the base of the forty-foot cliff where Bayani was positioned. His shaking hands fired at a darting shadow and missed. On each side of him, fifty yards apart, machine gun fire erupted sporadically. For the American and Filipino defenders, there was no lack of targets of opportunity. The Japanese were relentless.

After the initial frenzied exchange, the volume of fire slowed down. Both sides appeared to be running low on ammunition and were conserving their resources.

Bayani heard the dreaded order from the defenders' line: "Fix your bayonets!"

Far to his right, Clyde Bailey, a burly Marine master sergeant who replaced the recently fallen platoon commander, rose off his knees and clambered over the bulwark of earth fronting their dug-in position to repel the charge of the enemy.

Bayani and the others followed suit. In front of him, an enemy soldier, appearing winded from his climb up the cliff, emerged through a gap between two knee-high boulders. Behind him, another could be seen waiting his turn to climb to level ground.

The first soldier stared helplessly through muddy spectacles, as Bayani's rifle butt slammed into his nose. The impact sent him reeling backward into the man behind him.

Bayani pressed his advantage, shoving the off-balanced soldier with a vicious kick at the groin with a booted foot. The man behind saw the falling soldier about to land on him and tried to prop him up with one hand, but it was too late.

Bayani watched as the two Japanese soldiers hurtled down the cliff to the waiting rocks below.

The brief skirmishes along the line gave the enemy pause. The Japanese withdrew to the beach to await reinforcements and re-supply, since the defenders were not ready to quit.

The failed attack, with the first face-to-face look at their Japanese adversaries, gave Bailey and his men a measure of triumph. But they stifled their desire to celebrate; everyone knew it was only the beginning.

Not far away, silhouetted against the light of gunfire flashes, tracers, and burning barges, more attackers poured in from the sea. By early dawn, it became clear. The enemy numbers were slowly building, while the casualties of the defenders of Corregidor were not being replaced.

Sergeant Bailey looked at his signalman who tried in vain to reach his commanding officer on the phone. The line was dead. He looked up and down the line and fixed his eye on the soldier who had been fighting like a whirling dervish.

"Bayani, find the captain and inform him we are under heavy attack, our radio is dead, and we are in need of more men, ammo, and grenades."

It was less than a thousand yards to the captain's command post beyond the mouth of Malinta tunnel, but it was not a straight path; it was littered with shrapnel, empty shells, and ankle-breaking large pock marks of uneven ground.

Somehow, Bayani's luck continued to hold. He dove, darted, and scampered, sustaining minor multiple cuts on his arms and legs. At the command post the captain took Bayani's report and passed it on to his superior officer.

The colonel was in a quandary. What if this was just a feint on the enemy's part? If he sent reinforcements too soon, would they attack elsewhere along the line? His decided to hold. In the meantime, the captain would send in ammunition and grenades.

Bayani was stuck, unable to rejoin his unit. Around him men were mowed down as they tried to seek better fighting positions. Picture this: a hyena, one of the most vicious animals with a bite pressure of 1,100 pounds per square inch, enough to break the leg bone of a cow, becomes surrounded on all sides by a pride of lions. What does it do? It sits down to protect its most vulnerable part, its tail end. A seasoned lion would not dare chance a frontal confrontation.

By the same analogy, the Japanese decided to worry the tadpole's tail and work their way up, because it seemed to be the least defended and most vulnerable. Tactically, they were right. Six hours later, at dawn, the Japanese beachhead solidified at the tail end of the island. They brought better weapons, like the knee mortars that were efficient and accurate compared to the antiquated hand grenades of the beleaguered defenders. The enemy footprint slowly began to broaden with more troop landings and more intense firepower aimed at the defenders. The enemy gained ground and was now able to confront the men in the trenches.

It became hand-to-hand combat—the clang of steel on steel, the sharp rip of torn clothing and skin, the thud on impact of a rifle butt against breaking bone, the grunt and roar of the combatants fighting for their lives. Blood gushed freely, enemy blood mixed with defenders' blood dripped on the cold, indifferent earth trampled beneath their feet.

The US Marine commander heard the pleas for help and reinforcements, and there were many. The men in their foxholes at Topside heard the increasing din of the firefight at the Tadpole's tail and were frustrated at their inability to fight alongside their comrades.

The Marine colonel finally knew he had no option left but to send help by committing his reserves to the Tadpole's tail. He still kept the remainder of the defenders on the head and body and hoped for the best.

Bayani guided the reserve company sent to help Sergeant Bailey's beleaguered men. By this time, withering fire from the Japanese troops who had slowly overrun most of the tail of the island made it difficult to make progress. He led the men down a shallow gully he had navigated safely earlier in the day, but it led to a great loss of men. Enemy sniper fire picked off most of the reserve company.

Bayani and the few survivors who got through the ambush picked up ammunition and grenades cached around the tunnel and kept going toward the tail. But they could not inch farther beyond the outer trenches around the mouth of Malinta tunnel, the heart of the central headquarters of the army, where the wounded and the sick were sheltered.

The enemy had already overrun most of the lower island, including a gun emplacement called Denver battery. The welter of firing was endless. The deafening sounds of thousands of rounds fired by desperate and brave men on both sides, almost blended as one.

At daybreak, the Japanese not only had landed, they had also gained a foothold on the beach. More men came ashore; so did the dreaded tanks!

The booming shots, one after another from enemy tanks that had successfully landed, were like the grand finale at a fireworks display on Independence Day. The American and Filipino defenders could not match them and became overwhelmed. It was demoralizing. Denver battery absorbed heavy blows from the tank cannons and Japanese mortars and had to close up shop. The tanks began aiming at the hillside covering Malinta tunnel.

Bayani fired his rifle relentlessly at the enemy who was now less than half a football field from his defensive position. There was no dearth of targets. The Japanese were pouncing from everywhere like an army of ants. In front of him was a growing pile of enemy bodies from Bayani's rifle shots. He had no need to aim. Just point and shoot. The barrel of his rifle was red-hot to his touch. Running out of bullets, he found a box of grenades that he lobbed as fast as he could pull the firing pins. The enemy was now less than twenty-five yards away.

A few hours later, they were joined by what was left of the soldiers defending the Tail of the Tadpole. There was no place else to go, no place left to hide. Behind them only a few yards lay the opening to the tunnel, the central command post, with General Wainwright and the wounded men.

It wasn't much: just a sharp poke in his rib and a scalding sensation in his throwing arm that shoved him forward. Bayani fell face down on the bloodied earth, his eyes staring at a dismembered arm and a twitching hand that held a live grenade only inches from his face. He reached to grab it, but couldn't. He tried once more, but failed. His arm was gone, the dismembered extremity in front of him being his own.

Then the grenade exploded. The last thing Bayani saw was a cloud of smoke. He smelled the odor of cordite and burning meat before passing into oblivion.

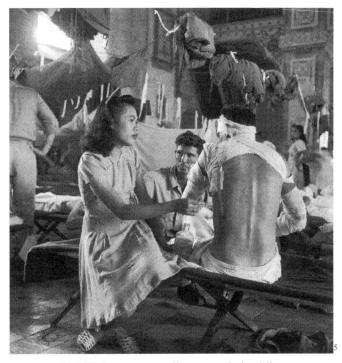

12-Filipino nurse tending wounded soldiers

A Marine major, blood covering his uniform, dusty carbine in hand, strode into the hospital section and asked for volunteers. The defenders were now only several feet away from the Malinta tunnel entrance. Those less-injured casualties who could still wield a

---

[5] W.Eugene Smith, Getty Images—https://www.gettyimages.com

firearm rose from their beds, picked up their weapons, and went to join their comrades in the raging battle.

On their way out, they passed the medics, badly wounded themselves, bringing in more injured and disabled. The hospital ward was awhirl with activity. The medical crew gave intravenous drips and applied dressings on injuries impossible to patch. There was no time to suture some bleeding wounds, and the lesser wounded in the next stretcher slid a hand to help. Cries of anguish emanated from the throats of those severely injured, especially those who had been burned or had lost a limb. Dead soldiers were carried directly to a holding area in the back of the adjoining tunnel, then laid in rows on the bare floor. More casualties replaced them in the still-bloody unmade beds that had just been vacated.

An hour later, the same Marine major, blood all over his shirt and bleeding from fresh wounds on his face and chest, went back into the tunnel and asked for more volunteers. Many tried to rise and groped for their firearms.

General Jonathan Wainwright had seen enough. He waved his hand to belay the order. Once the Japanese soldiers gained entry into the tunnel, there was apparently no doubt in his mind that every single man would be killed where they lay or stood.

He wrote a message sent by radio to Washington, D.C., of the inevitable decision to surrender, adding, "Enough sacrifices had been made."

The defenders of Bataan played music on the outside loudspeakers, a pre-arranged signal of surrender. At the battlefield outside of Malinta tunnel, it was as if a curtain had been dropped. Gunfire sputtered and finally ceased.

At the moment of surrender, General Wainwright did not come out. He ordered two American commissioned officers, to march out of the tunnel bearing the white flag. They waded through ankle-deep, still-warm brass shells. Amid the debris were bodies of dead soldiers, dismembered limbs, and other body parts. Bomb craters from the flurry of combat only yards from the mouth of the tunnel marred the pockmarked earth. The smell of spilled blood, burning flesh, the hazy smoke of exploded ordnance, and settling dust permeated the atmosphere. The din of the deafening shriek of a thousand fireworks ceased as if an electric switch had turned it off.

The vanquished defenders broke their rifles against the rocks so they would not be of use to the victors. The artillery men sabotaged the remaining cannons with explosive charges. At the gun batteries, the surviving artillery men chiseled off the coordinates of would-be targets written on the flat concrete slabs near the gun mounts to prevent the enemy from using them.

The commanding colonel ordered the flag of the United States Marine Regiment and its records be burned to avoid their being used as victory propaganda by the Japanese.

The American flag, flying aloft on its flagpole at Topside of the island, was taken down by the triumphant Japanese amid raucous shouts of *Banzais*.

General Wainwright, in his rumpled khaki uniform and unbuttoned collar, emerged and surrendered to a Japanese lieutenant colonel, who put Wainwright and his staff on a boat to Bataan. Corregidor had surrendered, but that was not enough.

At the place of formal surrender at Bataan, General Wainwright awaited the arrival of the Japanese commander, General Masaharo Homma. There was no formal exchange of pleasantries. Wainwright, six foot plus, 160 pounds, wearing the same dirty khakis since the battle began, sat at one side with a plain walking cane beside him. He and a few members of his staff sat across the rectangular table from Homma, the five foot ten, two hundred pound, bemedaled general dressed in olive green, with an open white shirt, plus a sword. Homma demanded that a radio message be sent to all units in the Philippines to cease hostilities, not just in Corregidor and Bataan. Under the veiled threat of harm to the prisoners of war, General Wainwright was left with only one choice.

He issued an order broadcast hourly on the radio waves of the Voice of Freedom to all the American and Filipino soldiers to lay down their arms.

Sergeant Powell, Kehaya's sergeant, was far ahead of the anticipated order of the surrender broadcast. Armed with sledgehammers, his men smashed all vital radio and telegraphic equipment save for one. When the Japanese took over, they did not notice anything was amiss because the cabinets were intact and the lights and dials were in place. Even the floor had been meticulously swept clean of any evidence of demolition activity. Piles of Philippine Commonwealth currency totaling two million pesos, equivalent to one million US dollars were hurriedly cut up with scissors by the Americans, rendering them worthless.

-o-

The demands for surrender were in reality obeyed in only a few key islands. Out of the forty-eight provinces only twelve were under Japanese occupation, mostly in the Province of Luzon. Guerillas formed and flourished even more so after the atrocities by the Japanese on the civilians and its captured Filipino soldiers became known.

An invisible staying hand bade them wait for the opportune time to strike back. Time was needed to regroup and re-arm.

It would take a couple of years.

Close to four thousand of the badly injured soldiers from Corregidor were taken to Manila, where they were interned at University of Santo Tomas University campus, which had a hospital. Hundreds more were imprisoned in the bleak dungeons at the ancient Spanish Fort Santiago inside Intramuros. The remainder of the prisoners of war were sent to various prison camps on the island of Luzon at Cabanatuan and Tarlac, and on the adjoining islands in Mindoro and Palawan.

More than one thousand of the captured men from Corregidor, those uninjured or with minor injuries, were marched to Manila to be confined at Bilibid Prison. There they were packed six to twelve men to a cell among the hard core Filipino prisoners sentenced to serve their time for the worst criminal offenses before the war began.

General Wainwright was force marched to the internment camp at Capas, Tarlac. He was not accorded treatment befitting his rank. Like everyone else, he was made to bow in front of lowly privates, noncommissioned officers, and officers below flag rank. From the internment camp, he was loaded on a ship to work in various military installations in Formosa. Before war's end, he and the men interned with him were brought to Manchuria until the Russian army liberated them.

Sergeant Powell and radioman Vince Kehaya were sent to Bilibid Prison for internment

13-Bataan Death March
On April 2, 1942, 80,000 soldiers—12,000 Americans and 68,000 Filipinos, a ratio of one American to twelve Philipinos—surrendered to the Japanese Army. Many died on the seventy kilometer journey on foot to internment camps. [6]

---

[6] Photo purchased from AP Images. https://www.apimages.com/

Death March

Why would one not call it the March of Death?

There was no other way to describe the slaughter. Every kilometer of the journey from the fields of battle at Bataan and Corregidor to the prison camps of places like O'Donnell and Cabanatuan was littered with the corpses of men who could no longer move on. They had been hampered by war wounds, disease, hunger, or the physical and mental stress of months in open trenches awaiting the sound of incoming cannon fire and bombs. Years after the war, survivors still flinched or shuddered at the loud reports and sharp sounds reminiscent of their harrowing experiences. This condition of shell shock in a now clinically recognized as Post-traumatic stress disorder.

To not be the recipient of a missile that could kill you on any given day of the war was like winning the lottery. Therein lay the sad irony. Most of those who survived as combatants died as non-combatants—prisoners of war.

In an attempt to be fair, one can say the slow pace of the march probably taxed the patience of the Japanese guards and forced them to do the inevitable: kill the weak, leave no survivors behind.

They shot and killed the POWs, clubbed them with rifles and pistols, or stabbed them with bayonets. The officers, who had swords, made the unlucky prisoners kneel with heads bowed and, in one stroke, beheaded them. This act may appear barbaric to the Westerner, but to the Japanese warrior, decapitation is the honorable way of the *samurai.*

120

Along the journey, the prisoners were occasionally marched off the road into an open field to allow a Japanese column of tanks, trucks, and marching men priority to pass in the opposite direction toward Manila.

POWs not agile enough to move off the road were trampled under the feet of Japanese in parade formation like marching wooden soldiers, eyes straight ahead, not daring to deviate lest they incur the wrath of their superior officers sternly watching them.

Worst of all, the tanks and trucks ran over bodies dead or barely alive, littering the ground with spilled blood and guts. Japanese officers on horseback scorned the POWs. They intentionally trampled the fallen bodies with the hooves of their horses.

Some of the men drank the muddy water from the *carabao* wallows, where water buffaloes cooled their bodies. Captain Toribio observed a fellow prisoner several feet away who groped to drink the last few drops of precious water from his canteen. A Japanese guard swatted it away in a sadistic gesture with the butt of a rifle, knocking out several of the prisoner's front teeth in the process.

Barok, the school janitor, vividly recalled having to pee on his shirtsleeve so he could suck on the moisture to wet his mouth. He remembered visual images of crazed thirsty prisoners making a mad dash off the road at the sight of a nearby spring or gushing well. Those who broke off the column were brutally beaten, stabbed, or shot. He did not want to make that mistake.

After baking in the hot sun for hours, when the long column of soldiers and tanks had passed, the POWs were ordered back on the road again. It would seem reasonable to assume that the rest would give them a second wind, but it wasn't so. Despite taunts, due to physical beatings many found it impossible to rise. More men perished. Dead bodies lay strewn along the path of the march.

Burial was done *en masse* in common graves. Out of necessity, the graves at Prison Camp O'Donnell were dug outside

121

the barbed wire enclosure. Burial details to carry the dead outside the gate were picked at all hours of the day and early evening. As the burial pits overflowed, mass graves were dug farther from the line of sight of the sentries in the towers.

14-Captured soldiers carrying their dead comrades
in makeshift litters to mass graves dug outside the internment camp. [7]

In the early evenings, the Japanese soldiers grew slipshod and careless. They left the graves to be covered with earth till the next day fearful of straying away from the camp enclosure for too long. And they didn't keep a head count on the burial parties coming and going.

Barok took mental notes of this observation and came up with a daring escape plan. One moonless night when he was picked to help carry one of the dozen corpses outside the fence, he waited for the guard nearest him to turn his attention elsewhere. Choosing the right moment, Barok wrapped his arms around the dead weight

---

[7] Photo from the National Archive. https://www.archives.gov/

he was carrying and slid with the corpse into the open grave, his figure melting in the dark pit. At midnight, he crawled out and headed for the hills. He entered a farmer's hut and begged for help. Not wanting to have to explain to the Japanese should they be looking for Barok, the farmer was only too glad to lead him away that same night to the safety of the forest. Barok worked his way back to Bisal, his hometown, two months later.

When the schools were re-opened by the Japanese during the two years of occupation, he resumed his work as the school janitor, where he served as the eyes and ears for the local guerillas hiding in the nearby mountain.

Escape to the Mountain

Toribio willed himself to stand unaided. To appear helpless could mean his death. The guards were relentless, tired, and less tolerant. He tried to focus and think. He knew he would not survive this journey without keeping his wits.

Gonzalo, ever ready to assist, solicitously watched his Patron out of the corner of his eye. Noticing the steely stare in Toribio's eyes and the way he blinked, he perceived something was afoot. He made sure to stay close by his side. Toribio mumbled a few words in Gonzalo's ear before breaking off.

About a kilometer ahead of them, a hill rose to accommodate a culvert for a dry stream bed running under the road. On either side of the road, dead soldiers lay in various states of repose, no longer able to scale the incline. Many bore visible wounds from gunshots or bayonet stabs on their exposed backs. Faces stared at the sky, eyes unseeing, their frozen expressions calm in death.

Stench was everywhere—from the rapid decay of spoiling flesh in the hot tropical sun and the involuntary release of body fluids upon death. Flies drawn by the scent converged by the thousands.

The Japanese guard nearest to Captain Toribio turned his head, annoyed by a growing gap in the slow-moving column that now stretched for several kilometers. Something was holding up the line. The guard retraced his steps to see two men abreast holding a man between them gasping for air from a chest wound.

Toribio nudged Gonzalo sharply in the ribs. On cue, Gonzalo shoved his master as hard as he could toward the embankment.

Toribio pushed with his good leg and somersaulted, chin tucked to his chest, knees flexed, his body a tight ball.

Gathering momentum, he rolled over and over before coming to a stop at the base of the hill. He found himself face down on the ground against a stack of bodies. He nosed his way under the corpses but somehow could only hide his head and shoulders, leaving the rest of his body exposed. His bad hip throbbed. He gritted his teeth to stifle a moan.

Motionless, he awaited the fateful shot that would decide if he was going to live or die.

Toribio heard the sound of rifle fire, but it was not meant for him.

The guard never saw Toribio fall off the embankment. He had just shot the sick man who was cast aside by the two Samaritans, when the soldier moved threateningly toward them.

The sound of shooting urged the prisoner line to move with renewed vigor away from the threat. Crossing the culvert, they came to a bend. Here, crowds from town gathered by the side of the road to look for a familiar face among the passing prisoners. An old woman asked in a barely audible voice for news of a loved one.

Gonzalo glanced surreptitiously behind him and noticed that the Japanese soldier was not in sight. He saw his chance.

Darting off the road, he headed toward the surprised crowd that parted and closed ranks quickly to shield him from view. On all fours, he saw a woman's ankle-long skirt, which he lifted over his head like a shroud and wrapped his trembling hands around her legs. Silently, he implored her not to give him away. The surprised woman tottered uncertainly but did not scream or run. Two people on either side of her held her up with braced shoulders.

Hours later, at dusk, the crowd slowly dispersed. Gonzalo, obscured in their midst, stayed with them before melting away in the tree line beyond.

Gonzalo waited until nightfall before crawling back in the direction of the culvert. He found Toribio among the pile of bodies exactly where he thought he would be.

They crawled on their bellies most of the night evading the roads still thick with enemy soldiers in makeshift tents, talking in their guttural accent. Three nights later, they came upon the pitted terrain of the battlefields of Bataan where they had started their march of surrender. Hopping over trenches and dead bodies, Gonzalo found a rifle half buried in the upturned soil.

As he clawed in the dark with his bare hands to unearth the rest of the weapon, he felt a detached forearm with the forefinger still on the trigger. Revulsed, he let go of the rifle, wrung his hands, and retreated to the far end of the bomb crater.

Captain Toribio had finished scavenging in the nearby foxhole. He emerged holding a clip of unfired rifle ammunition, a knapsack, two empty water canteens, two tins of canned food, and a .45 caliber handgun with holster. All taken from around a dead officer's waist.

Gonzalo took the first watch while his captain slept. He kept awake by making good use of his time. Disregarding his loathing for the still attached finger of its previous user, he dug up and cleaned the rifle. When the night was still at its darkest, both men, feeling rested, slithered out of the foxhole and headed in the direction of the looming mountain.

Captain Toribio had trouble maintaining his footing on the pockmarked landscape. In the dark, he blundered into a dead body causing him to sprawl. Breaking his fall with outstretched hand, he made contact with a dismembered arm that rolled away like a log into a nearby depression.

Body parts were everywhere, a common consequence of cannon shell bursts, Toribio observed.

Gonzalo inwardly felt concerned about Toribio's ability to finish the journey. He carried most of the load, leaving the captain with his sidearm, poncho, and canteen.

At daybreak, they rested within sight of a solitary farmer's hut but chose to stay hidden in a clump of dense vegetation. They bathed in a nearby rill, the flowing mountain water so clear they saw small snails and little clams, which they ate raw. They drank, filled their canteens, and dressed Toribio's wound from a medical kit.

Night became their ally. They headed toward the mountain following a faint white outline of a foot trail. Hours later, they entered the forest. Here, it was suddenly cool and even darker. The ambient light from the stars was no longer able to show them the way. They moved deep into the foliage, shared the last tin of food ration between them, laid their heads on the spread poncho on the ground, and were out like a light within seconds.

At dawn, a bird plucked a worm out of the ground a few feet away from their heads. The forest awoke with the flutter of bird wings stretching prior to taking off in search of a meal. None of these was heard by the sleeping forms of the weary men.

A beam of sun pierced the leafy canopy and awakened Toribio. He kicked Gonzalo's boots roughly as he rolled up his poncho.

They followed the trail leading up the mountain without pause over the next three hours. A large rock with an outcropping of shrubs offered concealment.

While they rested, Gonzalo continued to forage for fruit. The familiar leaf of the sago plant made him smile. Digging at the root, he found several of the starch-rich tubers. They ate them unpeeled, their first fresh vegetable in months.

They would have to survive on small game and fruit until they reached home.

Each day, they traveled a few kilometers, always following a northerly course parallel to and just below the spine of the mountain.

There the trees and shrubbery did not seem to thrive as much, thus they could make better time. But the route had a drawback: it did not offer much concealment. Once they caught sight of three soldiers silhouetted against the backdrop of the blue sea and sky ahead of them. So they sought the lower mountain where the forest could hide them, albeit at the price of traveling at a slower pace.

Gonzalo was in the lead as he had been since they left Bataan. They followed faint animal trails that intersected and switched every now and then. If one was not careful, it was easy to take a path that circled back causing them to lose time and distance.

They had been on the move for at least three weeks and were becoming impatient to reach their destination. Although the captain seemed to be mending each day, Gonzalo felt responsible for his safe return home.

By his reckoning, the monsoon season would be upon them any day. May 1942 had seen sporadic showers. The sticky clay on the mountain trails caked on the soles of their boots, making them annoyingly heavy.

He had removed his combat boots and strapped them to his backpack, then walked surefootedly on the sometimes-slippery slope of mud and grass. As a farmer inured to hard work in muddy rice paddies, shoes and boots were an impediment in knee-deep muck and water. He trusted the feel of his soles and toes to give him proper traction and balance in such an element.

Gonzalo suddenly stopped, pointing to a specimen on the side of the trail.

"Wild boar turd. About five hours old."

Both men knelt, studying the spoor, their hunting senses keyed up. Gonzalo pointed down the mountain. The grass had bent and the ground was upturned where the pig had dug for grubs.

Each felt a rising anticipation. A meal of fresh meat would be a welcome change to the one-quarter rations of the past few months in Bataan and their meager meals of wild fruit and roots in the mountain.

Gonzalo sniffed at the wind and looked at the sun to see how much daylight remained.

Toribio, ever cautious, counseled, "Let's not get careless."

The spoor entered the edge of the leafy tree line at the bottom of the mountain. The dappled rays of the sun penetrated between the leaves overhead, causing mixed patterns and shadows on the tree branches and trunks. They paused to allow their vision to adjust.

One hundred yards away, they identified a *duhat*, a stately tree about fifty feet tall with dark broad leaves ripe with bunches of luscious deep purple fruit.

Gonzalo and Toribio dropped to a squat and did not move. The tree was alive with wild birds. Orioles flashed their yellow and black plumage. A flock of green parrots sat on the branches inspecting each fruit with a sideways look before plucking the chosen one. Little birds called *mayas*, tropical bright-colored birds no larger than sparrows, pecked delicately with their beaks at the soft skin of the ripe fruit, savoring each dainty bite.

A troop of monkeys, swinging from limb to limb with abandon, feasted greedily at the very top of the trees, stuffed their cheeks with fruit, and plucked more, although they could not eat them fast enough. In their haste they dropped hundreds of the ripe fruit to the ground, where other animals waited.

A rifle shot rang out as Gonzalo was about to move sideways to get into a better shooting position. Toribio pulled him to the ground and dragged him to cover. They looked ahead, their eyes swiveling, their heads and bodies still. The forest was suddenly silent. Every bird and animal had instantly disappeared.

"They haven't seen us or else they would not have fired at that," Toribio whispered. He pointed with his pursed lips at a dead pig, adding, "That sounded like a US carbine, not a Japanese rifle, don't you agree?"

Gonzalo concurred, nodding.

They split the area in half, Toribio continuing to stare ahead and to his right. Gonzalo turned his head slowly to cover their rear and to the left.

"American soldier," Toribio whispered, recognizing the uniform. His light skin was unmistakable. "He is moving toward the kill."

Visibly relieved that they did not blunder into the open, they remained hidden; after an hour, they withdrew.

It was better to go hungry than to be shot at by a man with a nervous trigger finger. Both felt relieved it wasn't *tulisan*, roving bandits in the hills and mountains.

The two men found their way back to their hometown of Bisal, but decided it was safer to hide out in the mountains.

15-Carromata, a horse drawn passenger vehicle
Used before WWII and even today although rarely..

Det

Det was stuck in Manila following her indecision as to what she should do. Two weeks after the Japanese bombing of Pearl Harbor, she finally packed her belongings, locked her front door for the last time, and stepped out into the street. Hefting her considerable luggage atop her head, she took off for the bus terminal several blocks away.

She realized she had made an untimely decision. No vehicles were available for hire at any price, probably because they were taken by the retreating army or had been hidden away by their owners. She put down her load and sat on the curb to wipe the sweat off her face. It was December 24, 1941.

Across the street, a woman named Ramona recognized her and waved frantically. She was one of Det's fellow schoolteachers.

"Where are you going? Why are you alone?" Ramona continued a tattoo of questions. "Haven't you heard the news? The Japanese may be only hours away from entering the city and the American forces have left for Bataan and Corregidor."

Det replied, "I know. It was announced over the radio before I left the house. I'm planning to go to my hometown in the province to rejoin my family. But," she swept her hand around them, "there is no transportation available."

Ramona spoke with a shudder. "Don't do it. It is so dangerous to be out on the streets and you will be heading in the path of the Japanese soldiers. Already, they have landed in Lingayen Gulf on the way to Manila."

Ramona was able to persuade Det to at least come to her house for a glass of water and to meet her family. Her husband, Marcial, a prosperous dentist, welcomed Det and introduced the three children and Ramona's mother.

During the conversation he said, "General MacArthur, before leaving for Corregidor with his army, has declared Manila an open city. Hopefully, the Japanese will enter and occupy Manila without having to fire a single bullet. So we are safe here where we are."

Ramona noticed the unease in Det's demeanor. "Why don't you stay with us at least a few days until things settle down a bit?"

Contrary to expectations, the Japanese army, skeptical of MacArthur's radio announcement, bombed Manila before occupying the city. Taking nothing for granted, the Japanese shelled the city sporadically for several more days.

Det and Ramona's family ate and slept in hastily dug foxholes beneath the house. During a lull in the shelling, Ramona and Det went upstairs to salvage whatever they could. Luck was with them. A few pots, pans, and cooking utensils were undamaged. Bullet holes had damaged part of the walls of the house; splintered picture frames, useless pieces of wood, lay on the floor. Water ran freely from broken pipes and plumbing.

They cooked food in the kitchen and took their meals to the foxholes. For their water supply, Marcial went next door to fill a large can from his neighbor's hand-operated artesian pump, which was surprisingly undamaged.

The Japanese cautiously entered Manila three weeks later. Marcial and the family discussed the situation. Food would soon become a scarce commodity and their personal safety was an increasing cause for concern.

The family held a hasty conference and decided to evacuate their home when it was appropriate—but to where?

Marcial suggested the farm of his father's cousin, Tio Juan, about sixty kilometers south of the city, a place which, as a boy, Marcial had frequented with his parents. Quietly, they started to pack.

Only their essential belongings were to be taken. Ramona noted the undamaged religious icon on the wall—a miracle! She decided to take it with them.

Marcial found a large earthen jar where he stored most of his valuables and the papers and title to their property, then buried it in a corner of the yard. He piled a mound of rubbish over the jar to hide it from roaming thieves. He took gold coins and items of jewelry on his person. He could use them for barter or as a bribe in case they were confronted along their journey.

Tomas, his next door neighbor, had been watching all the activity from his side of the fence and guessed something was afoot. He loudly inquired. Marcial had no choice but to tell him. Tomas begged to come along with his wife and children.

They left in mid-morning. Marcial and Tomas took turns moving ahead a block at a time reconnoitering the area ahead of them.

All seemed well until they came to an intersection patrolled by two Japanese soldiers. A *carromata,* a horse-drawn two-wheeled vehicle able to carry up to six passengers, blundered into the open square before the farmer driving it realized the presence of the soldiers. He was ordered to stop. One soldier poked randomly with his bayonet at the cartful of ripe watermelons.

In the increasing heat and humidity, Marcial, watching from a distance, felt a sudden thirst, salivating at the sight of red watermelon juice dripping on the ground, but he remained out of sight. The farmer took the initiative and slowly handed a melon to one of the soldiers who grabbed it and motioned harshly for the farmer to move along. Gratefully, he whipped his horse in the direction of the local market. He had taken an enormous risk, but his fruit was getting overripe. He had to sell them that day.

In late afternoon, a military truck, the open back half filled with sentries who had just finished their shifts patrolling various intersections, came by to collect the two soldiers. Within minutes, the unguarded intersection became busy with foot traffic as if every civilian had been watching, biding their time waiting to cross.

Along came Det with one of Ramona's younger daughters, who, in innocent bliss and oblivious to the potential danger, hopped and skipped alongside Det as they crossed the street.

Det wore an ankle-long skirt purse-stringed around her waist and a loose drab dress. A black headscarf tied at the neck, a short cane, and a *bayong,* a locally-woven straw bag, in the crook of her elbow completed her disguise as an old hag.

Dressed in old clothing and with stooped posture, Ramona followed a few yards back with her aging mother. Marcial and Tomas stuck to their plan. They traveled singly and with small groups. They maintained a separation until they reached the outskirts of the city where they were to rejoin their families.

At dusk as planned, the two families caught up with each other. They found a spot shaded by a large acacia tree and close to the road, and set up camp for the evening. For supper Ramona doled out sparse portions of dried fish and boiled rice in anticipation of a few more days of travel with no idea where the next meal would come from.

Early the next day, they set out to join a long procession of evacuees headed out of the city in search of safe haven. Many had no purpose or destination. Five hundred meters ahead, the line of people came to a bottleneck in the road.

Marcial craned his neck and listened to the buzz of news filtering from the people ahead. There was a five-soldier Japanese checkpoint before entry into the main thoroughfare of the next town. Moving off the side of the road as if to sit on a rock, he discerned an armed civilian among the Japanese soldiers. A handkerchief was tied behind his ears and covered his face: a Filipino collaborator already working for the Japanese military! Scanning the passing crowd, he gestured to the soldiers who occasionally ferreted out a person from the crowd, usually a male.

Marcial's mind went into overdrive. This was not good. He spoke to Ramona, who had surreptitiously removed a leather purse of jewelry and gold coins tied by a string around her neck and nestled between her breasts. She handed it to Marcial, who hid it in a secret pocket of his waistband. He in turn thought about his appearance: he saw the gold wedding band around his finger and swiftly removed it. What else? He remembered the two gold dental caps in his mouth! Quickly, he removed them as well.

He glanced in Tomas' direction. He was whimpering softly, his shoulders shook as if from the cold. Marcial nudged him roughly and whispered.

"It is a checkpoint. They are going after the men who are being picked out by that Filipino traitor with the handkerchief mask. The women and children will be fine."

Marcial looked about and saw a soldier going down the line of people. He pulled Tomas to the opposite side of the road and casually turned to relieve his bladder against a fence post.

There! His roving eyes saw a small stack of hay. Casually, he moved slowly in an oblique direction so as not to attract any attention, screening himself from the line of sight of the soldier. Tomas followed discretely behind. Neither one looked back, just a casual stroll like two men poking around for a place to do their personal business in private. They sat in a stony pose behind the screen of hay, not moving for hours.

It worked. Even the people passing by failed to notice them. When the shadows of dusk came, they rose and left. But they did not take the road. They skirted the town and kept on a southerly course. Marcial smelled water and a cooling breeze. That would be the lake where his uncle took him and his father out boating. Not much farther, he turned away from the lake. A familiar mango tree came into view. It was about fifty feet high with a long thigh-sized branch dipping just three feet above the ground like a giant's muscular arm.

At the sight of a dirt path that entered a grove of coconut trees, he remembered the early years of his boyhood when he ran and played here. He looked ahead. Tio Juan's house should be in the shadows of those now overgrown acacia trees. The house was empty. No barking dogs. No one responded to their call.

Tomas wanted to go back and find his wife and family; he needed to know what happened to them. Reason prevailed. It was late, they were tired and hungry, and they could get lost in the inky darkness of the countryside where there was no electricity.

They moved to the back of the yard and found the granary enclosed on all sides and sheltered by a leaning canopy of thatched nipa palm leaves supported by two bamboo poles. Beneath, two rice pestles rested on the ground next to a long wooden mortar and a hollowed-out trunk of a tree used for threshing and pounding the rice grain from the stalk and husk. The men sat inside the hollow, faced each other, laid down their heads against the opposite ends of the mortar, and were out like lights.

Each day, Tio Juan came back to the house in the early morning with his wife, daughter, and her two children. Not with the family was his son-in-law, an enlisted soldier with the Philippine Scouts, who had brought his family to the farm before going off, as ordered, to fight the war against the invading Japanese at Bataan.

For added safety, Tio Juan had his farmhands build him a roofed shelter, open at the sides, with a raised platform of bamboo. They left the house every night to sleep at the shelter stocked with provisions on the mountainside a few kilometers away from his home. Every morning, they rose early and made breakfast before returning to their home.

Today, something seemed amiss. His dogs that normally meandered in and out of the trail sniffing and spraying their urine scent to mark their territory stiffened their backs, furrowed their foreheads, and pinned back their ears as they came within sight of the house.

Tio Juan cautioned his family to conceal themselves, while he advanced to get a better view. The two dogs went at random about the yard until they picked up a spoor. Unerringly, they headed for the granary shed just sniffing, not barking.

Marcial's hand was dangling loosely off the side of the wooden mortar when the whiskers of the sniffing dog touched Marcial's skin causing him to twitch involuntarily. The surprised dog lurched back and barked, quickly joined by the other dog, waking both men. Marcial rose and looked around. Back in the bush, Tio Juan studied Marcial's features. It was unmistakable. He ran out of hiding, a wide grin on his face. In the moment of recognition, the two kin shook hands. Marcial, remembering his place in the hierarchy as nephew, bowed, took Tio Juan's hand again, and pressed it to his lips in a gesture of deference.

Tio Juan showed signs of aging with strands of gray hair along his temples, yet he looked fit. He regarded his nephew, who appeared a little paunchy, but this was not unusual for a city mouse who does little manual work, he thought.

Tio Juan guffawed when he noticed his nephew's missing teeth; knowing that he was a dentist by trade, he chided Marcial playfully about it. The embarrassed Marcial retrieved his gold caps out of his pocket, restored them to their rightful place, and smiled again. Tio Juan nodded approvingly.

Now it was time for serious business. Marcial introduced Tomas and briefly explained the reason for their visit, which might last for an indefinite period. Over a quick breakfast, Tio Juan listened to the recounting of each one's individual adventures and experiences in the invasion of Manila and recent travel to leave the city.

It was obvious that the first priority was to find the families of Marcial and Tomas. Tio Juan told his wife to summon one of his farmhands, who came with a water buffalo hitched to a sled. The men walked to the main road, remarkably not far away if one knew the shortcut. Two kilometers later, the men saw the approaching group of tired children and women. They loaded the sled with their belongings. Those too tired to walk took turns riding in the slow-moving sled. The others walked back to Tio Juan's farm.

Det was unable to rejoin her family for the duration of the Japanese occupation, which lasted two years. Ramona's family took her in unconditionally. While she lived at Tio Juan's house, she helped with the daily chores. In the evenings she applied her teacher skills and told bedtime stories of Jack and the Beanstalk, Goldilocks and the Three Bears, and the like, which endeared her to the children. One particular story that left them spellbound was Gulliver's Travels, about a sailor in a shipwreck who was found unconscious on the shore of an island inhabited by very tiny people called the Lilliput. Never having seen a man this big before and not knowing if he would be harmful to them, upon the order of their King. they decided to immobilize him. When Gulliver regained consciousness a few days later, every hair was fastened with thread and pins hammered to the ground. This included the fringes of his clothing effectively mobilizing his hands and feet. The children cringed in fright at this image of a giant, so the ending of this bedtime story was never told.

During the day, Ramona, Det, and Tomas's wife pounded rice sheaves on the wood mortar with three-foot-long wooden pestles to separate the stalk. Once done, the unhusked rice was transferred to a large round stone mortar and again pounded with pestles. This separated the husk to expose the rice grain. Finally, husk and grain were poured into a winnowing basket called *bilao* from whence the basket's contents were thrown a few inches in the air against a blowing wind. This would separate chaff from the now ready-to-cook grain.

It was a tedious process. The rice pounders made the drudgery tolerable by occasionally changing the cadence of the pounding and by humming a song.

In my mother's family, this activity had a tragic outcome. When she was in her early teens, one of my mother's sisters, Violeta, while pounding on the stone mortar with her wooden pestle, tried to push some of the spilled unpounded grain into the open bowl with her free hand, while three others were still pounding in a cadence. One of her fingers was accidentally crushed. She never had it treated. A few weeks later she died following a fever and infected finger. The town doctor attributed her death to tetanus.

Food was scarce, but daring vendors from nearby towns who farmed and fished near Tio Juan's farm ventured to sell their wares in Manila. It paid a little more, albeit in Japanese paper money, none of which was legal tender.

In the two years of the Japanese occupation, paper currency was printed and circulated. However, wise Filipinos shunned it, preferring barter in kind or purchase of goods using precious metals of gold, silver, and copper. Following the end of the Japanese occupation, many Filipinos were left holding bags of worthless Japanese paper currency. My own parents sold a small parcel of land in the latter currency at a loss after the war ended.

Ramona and Det would get up early and travel toward the road leading to the lake where the fishermen unloaded the night's catch to waiting fish vendors eager to rush to the nearest market before the fish spoiled.

They paid with one peso gold coins, silver dimes, and *pesetas* in Philippine currency, which was highly acceptable to the merchants who offered them a better selection of whatever they were able to purchase.

Matches and Embers

1943-44 was the year of want, the year of the Japanese occupation. Despite efforts by the Japanese conquerors to restore a semblance of normalcy, promising independence for the islands, re-opening of schools, printing of paper currency, and organization of a new government structure, life to the average Filipino wasn't the same. Farming, fishing, and commerce proceeded at an uncomfortable pace, which felt restrictive.

Farmers planted just enough to sustain themselves for lack of incentive. Barter was preferred to selling produce paid in Japanese paper currency. For instance, it cost the buyer a bag load of "Japanese money" to persuade a farmer to part with his kilo of uncooked rice.

It was hard on the families who lived in the densely populated towns and cities and depended on produce brought in from farms and meat raised in the countryside. Toward the latter part of the Japanese occupation, there were stories of people resorting to eating rats and dogs.

To stretch the food supply, my family mixed a cup of rice with an equal amount of ground corn before cooking. One of our neighbors, Lydia, a widow with three children, occasionally begged us for a cup of rice to cook.

Polonia was an old widow who lived alone in a tiny one-room nipa hut on the edge of town. She generally kept to herself and hardly spoke to anyone. I do not think she was as reclusive as most of the townspeople thought, because when I ran into her, I would give her a faint smile and got a wave in return. I tend to think that her social shortcoming was a consequence of her slightly grotesque appearance. Her thin physique, long face, and straight dark hair were marred by a sunken right nostril caused by an unknown injury at birth. People called her *Kutleng*, an aphorism for "bashed in nose."

Having no visible source of income, it is a wonder she managed to survive. Polonia Kutleng went to the bank of the river every day, usually in the same place beside a large shady tree with branches that spread out over the water causing a dark shadow most of the day. Brush and tall grass grew along the bank around it. Polonia would part the bushes carefully and walk toward the water's edge to squat on the tree root beneath her bare feet. No one would know she was there, because she was normally quiet, hardly moved, and wore the same old drab peasant's clothes.

Most of the day, she spent hours fishing using a meter-long stick with a long string attached at the end, an endeavor she must have enjoyed immensely. Beyond the string was a tiny fish hook that was bent out of a regular sewing needle. How she kept the barb sharp is hard to imagine, because one would need a microscopic set of tools to keep it that way.

She generally caught minnows. Not a lot, but they augmented her diet of edible vegetable leaves and an occasional bowl of rice. In peace or wartime, her diet hardly varied, so during the war, Polonia's life probably never felt impacted.

In the years of the Japanese Occupation, Polonia was recruited by the guerillas. Every day she sat on a flat rock at her favorite fishing hole and kept her eyes and ears open for ongoing traffic on the bridge: number of trucks, loads carried, soldiers coming and leaving, especially visiting officers of rank conspicuous with the wide white lapel on their blouses and sheathed swords at their waists. She used various colored pebbles in a pile beside her to keep a record. If she had anything significant to report, she would leave the pebbles by a lone tree on her way home. A guerilla sympathizer would pick them up, and by sorting the stones by color, he knew what the traffic bore for the day or week.

Polonia could not make sense of the little task she had been assigned to do, but she did not seem to mind. Once a month, she was rewarded with a cupful of uncooked rice for her troubles. This was left at the drop point by her unseen benefactor.

Information gathering of troop movements and equipment and shipping was a vital cog in the eventual return of the American troops to liberate the country.

In some islands, guerilla resistance was more overt. Pity the Japanese patrols who dared to venture too far off base in the early months following the surrender of Bataan.

Ambushes were common. Whereas initially, Japanese, aided by Filipino collaborators, made lightning forays into suspected guerilla lairs, guerillas turned the tide on the patrols by sending in their spies—sometimes their own wives or children—into the town and setting up ambushes following receipt of this intelligence. This was not without repercussions. Civilians were rounded up, tortured, and often killed.

Captain Toribio made certain to be discrete about these attacks against the Japanese because of the consequences. He forbade any aggressive activity by the men under his control without his say so. The orders from the Americans supplying them with radios, food, and equipment were succinct: gather information for now. Do not confront. Wait.

From all over the Philippines, messages referencing the enemy were relayed by radio to offshore American submarines plying Philippine waters at night. They then transmitted the messages to General MacArthur's staff in Australia. This collated information helped the American and Filipino troops in saving thousands of lives in the Landing Zones at the time of the Liberation two years later.

The months of passivity did not sit well with a few guerillas. Eager for action, a small group purloined a few sticks of dynamite from the cache aside from their own firearms. They splintered away from the main band of guerillas and set up camp in a forest on the mountain about ten kilometers from Toribio's position.

To cloak his identity, the leader assumed a *nom de guerre*: *Buneng*, which stands for bolo or machete. Weeks later, he and three of his men, dressed as farmers, went to town separately carrying large baskets of vegetables headed for the marketplace. The market was fenced in with iron bars set in concrete. There were three gates of entry. Each gate was manned by two Japanese who stood on each side but did not stop the shoppers and vendors from entering.

By pre-arrangement, each man entered the marketplace via a different gate. Once inside the crowded market, they milled around aimlessly, seemingly undecided as to where to lay their wares. In the back end of the market was a stall with a Japanese flag atop it. There was plenty of room on the ground and around the stall, for who would want to set up shop close to the resting spot for the soldiers taking a break from their guard duty?

Under the shade of the stall, seven soldiers, at ease in conversation, sat or squatted on the ground. *Buneng* and the two men set up shop, displaying the vegetables in neat arrays on the spread cloth baskets. They made a fuss of breaking off browned leaves and dead stems while they waited for customers to come by. Less than an hour later, the soldiers made ready. The corporal roused them and headed out. It was time to relieve the soldiers at the gates who would return to rest in the shade of the stall.

Buneng started a silent count. Finally, he got up quite urgently and retreated to the back of the soldier's stall as if to answer a call of nature. Once out of sight, he reached inside his waist and pulled out a stick of dynamite. The other two men did the same in separate areas, planting their explosives as planned. Still counting mentally, he guessed the time the relieved soldiers would return. Each man lit his fuse and left. It was perfect timing. The corporal was just returning with his men.

Buneng and his men were already close to one of the side gates when the explosives blew. A sudden stampede of panicked shoppers quickly emptied the marketplace. There were upturned baskets of unsold produce. Japanese soldiers from the main garrison drove toward the almost deserted market, save for curious onlookers who were rounded up and subjected to harsh questioning from a Filipino collaborator.

Toribio was irate! What could possibly be accomplished with such a small token of resistance? But there was nothing he could do except damage control. He warned his men to inform their families to be on their toes.

Buneng paid for his impetuousness. Pressed by news that his name had finally emerged as the instigator of the market attack, he became a most wanted man. Japanese sent patrols in an effort to find him. He pulled his men to hide farther up the mountain away from the forest. This deprived him from hunting wild game needed to sustain his men. Farmers and sympathizers became reluctant to aid him in fear of retribution from the Japanese. Food became problematic. *Buneng* saw his starving men and noticed their ebbing morale. What could he do?

He came up with a plan. He picked three of his most reliable men and told the rest to wait while the four hunted for food. Six days later, they made their way back to camp with a sack load of red meat on each man's back. The hunters told the starving men it was venison, and the guerillas feasted that night with enough food left to last them for many days.

Buneng survived the war. In 1947, he published a short article in the weekly Philippines Free Press. Its title was "We Ate Jap Flesh." This writer actually read the article.

A fisherman fished only to supply his personal and bartering needs. It was like a boa constrictor squeezing its prey to a slow death.

Our family was fortunate to have chickens and eggs, a small herd of goats for their meat and milk, vegetables from our garden, and fruit from a small orchard.

We had the only matches in the neighborhood thanks to Nay's foresight in buying them before we boarded the train for home three years earlier. Live embers nursed in the ashes of our wood stove twenty-four hours a day stretched our match supply for three years during our period of need. We shared this resource with neighbors, who would take a precious glowing ember and fan it alive in a dried coconut husk, while rushing to their homes in time to light their own stoves.

We went out in the woods in search of edible fruit and wild mushrooms from time to time but weren't often successful. At the pond, we ate a variety of snail called *bilabil*, which did not have a protective shell. It must be agitated on a basin until it froths. It is believed that the frothy substance, if not removed before cooking, can make a person dizzy. It was at the bottom of our food chain, only to be eaten as a final resort.

In the final days before the Liberation, we resorted to eating boiled leaves of the sweet potato plant. They tasted like spinach. At the running rill, some purple tubers grew from the taro plant. Locally called *gabi*, when boiled and mashed, it was a good source of starch. As a child, I did not like the last one so much, because the rough stem going down my throat felt like swallowing fine sandpaper.

From our emergency supply, my parents saved the bag of flour bought at the store in Manila years ago before boarding the train. It was moistened with water into a thin patty for pancakes about three fingerbreadths across and pan fried in coconut oil. Only the children got it on their plates. There was no sugar or syrup available.

The Flood

I will rain down bread from heaven for you. Exodus 16:4

The wet season of 1944 came with a vengeance. It rained in endless sheets for days from the sea and over the peaks of the mountains close to the shore of Luzon. Rivulets merged and became running streams rushing down the slopes.

The river quickly filled beyond capacity. Its banks overflowed. Like a wild unruly serpent, the rushing water reared its head flicking its long tongue to probe for points of weakness. It tore the soil off the riverbank, exposing the roots of fully grown trees, then dragged them into the muddied swirling currents.

The Agno River Control Project was an ambitious government endeavor conceived before the war. It was meant to control the annual flooding of the fertile plains of the interior. Thousands of laborers, armed with picks and shovels and willing to work for a few pesos a day, loaded soil onto animal-drawn carts or used gurneys borne on the shoulders of two men to painstakingly build an earthen dike over a hundred kilometers long, parallel to the east side of the river.

Each year the same battle went on between the people living in Bisal and Mother Nature. With the occupation by the Japanese, dike maintenance and flood control were not at the top of their priorities. It could have averted the sequence of events that eventually happened.

Around the town of Bisal, the water serpent found a vulnerable section. It was an eroded depression devoid of grass or tree or shrubbery. Here the current gnawed away, at first taking small bites of soil. The townspeople noticed the early break, but there was nothing they could do but hope for the best. A gathering of people, although armed with shovels and loading carts, could be misconstrued wrongly by the Japanese as an uprising and lead to trouble.

A day later, the dike was breached.

I was lying in bed, cozy in a thin blanket, listening to the comforting soft patter of rain hitting the nipa-thatched roof. The closed bamboo-framed windows rattled gently from the gusting of wind coming from various directions as if it were trying to figure out the best way to blow the house down.

I had heard it before—the unmistakable gurgle of running water as it picks its way along rocks and pebbles in a slow-moving stream, filling up holes and depressions in the ground, evicting pockets of air into reluctant bubbles forced to the surface. Looking down at the spaces between the bamboo-slatted floor, I could see the ground beneath covered by gentle swirls of slowly rising water.

I then understood why homes in this part of the world are built on stilts.

Nay's wooden clog lazily floated by in my line of vision, followed by the empty food basin we normally used to feed the dogs.

I felt a rush of excitement and threw aside my blanket. Before I could get to the doorway, I heard Nay, who seemed to read my intent, give me a stern order.

"Stay inside the house."

I saw my aunts already outside, wading in the knee-deep water and carrying woven bamboo baskets and jute sacks. They were heading for the open town plaza where the terrain was elevated and the water only ankle deep.

Hundreds of *gourami* fish with black diamond-shaped scales measuring four fingerbreadths from dorsal to ventral fins were helplessly beached, thrashing, jumping, and spinning in a desperate attempt to find the sanctuary of deep water. Other townspeople were already there, exhorting members of their family to catch as much as they could of this unexpected bounty of food.

Esi and Mari scooped the *gourami* between their bare hands and threw the caught fish into their baskets. When these were filled, the fish were dumped in the jute sacks. Hungry birds, egrets, and herons took advantage of the lull in the wind and swooped down to fill their gullets.

That night was spent in the tedious task of gutting, scaling, cleaning, and salting the fish. We dried them in the sun the next day. By then the rain stopped; the flood had receded to the river.

That day's harvest amply sustained the town's food supply for weeks.

Saito

I woke one afternoon from my usual nap. It was a warm summer. A slanting ray of sunshine from the open bedroom window beat down on the bed. I was drenched in sweat. Looking to my right through the open doorway, I could see the dining room table and the kitchen beyond.

I saw the back of a man facing the wood stove, cooking, wearing short pants that reached mid-calf and a non-descript plain white cotton shirt. What was unforgettable was the extreme whiteness of the exposed legs and bare feet against his deeply tanned forearms, probably from wearing shoes and leggings everyday all day long as a soldier of the Japanese army.

I walked toward the covered balcony. Nay was busy pedaling away on her Singer sewing machine, working on a white cotton shirt, which judging by its size was obviously for me. It was almost finished. It had no collar and was sleeveless.

Noticing my presence, she motioned me over, took off my sweat-drenched shirt, and tried the new shirt on me for size.

It had two buttonholes but no buttons, for we had none. Instead, she had made two holes on the underlapping seam and skewered it with a wooden stick not much larger than a matchstick; the latter threaded through the button hole and anchored the front of the shirt closed.

Glancing at the foot of the stairs leading to the balcony, I noticed a strange pair of sandals among the neatly-arrayed wooden clogs of my mother, sisters, and aunts.

Only slippers were worn in the living space upstairs.

The man came out of the kitchen carrying a kidney-shaped tin can, his mess kit, on a handle. He bowed at the waist toward Nay and left as silently as he had come.

A small dish sat on the dining room table. The Japanese soldier in civilian clothes had left us some of the food he had just cooked.

We did not touch it. When Tay came home from the school, Nay told him about the off-duty soldier who had used the kitchen, then left.

Tay took out a spoon, tasted it, and ate the rest. We watched him but were reluctant to partake of this strange food.

A few weeks passed. My father had just harvested vine-ripened grape tomatoes from the garden. He has decided to sit awhile with us in the covered balcony. I reached inside the basket to grab a luscious tomato for myself.

Nay was busy mending a hole in the heel of one of Tay's socks. She had unscrewed a electric bulb off a light fixture and stuffed the bulb in the heel as a form. I watched, fascinated, as she patched the tear by making a spider web pattern using needle and thread unraveled from an old cotton-knit sock.

The same man, again in civilian clothing, came up quietly in his bare feet, having left his wood sandals at the foot of the stairs. He bowed deep, holding his mess kit *cum* cooking pot, obviously requesting permission to cook.

On the side of his kit were Japanese letterings and the hand-etched drawing of a fish's head and spine.

Nay and Tay displayed no sign of animosity, in fact welcomed him. Tay offered him some of the tomatoes. Gratefully, he accepted, bowing so low his head came down to my height.

Tay knew some basic Japanese since he was the school principal and was mandated to teach the students to learn the language. The two men conversed briefly, aided by sign language.

His name was Saito. He pointed at the Japanese lettering to indicate the meaning of the scrawl on his cooking appliance and to his chest. As a civilian, his family scaled fish at the market for a living, hence the fish-spine drawing etched on his mess kit.

Looking back over the years, bereft of his military accoutrements, in his sandals and peasant clothing, his frail countenance, I remember him looking vulnerable just like one of us, somewhat forlorn and, yes, homesick for a home-cooked meal and perhaps missing his family.

Saito, Japanese soldier, from a family of fish scalers.

Water Boarding

"Pick six men from the list," ordered the newly arrived intelligence officer of the Japanese. He had been sent on short notice to Bisal with orders to return the next day to the larger garrison in Mangalem five kilometers away. Guerilla activity had increased around Bisal, and the Japanese were becoming increasingly aware and annoyed.

Mysterious flooding of roads outside of town in the dry season had been impeding Japanese troop movements as they marched on patrols. A spy for the Japanese had insinuated it was intentional, caused by the resistance movement breaching sections of the retaining wall holding the water in the irrigation ditches to the rice fields.

It was almost 6 p.m., just before the pealing of the church bells to announce the angelus.

A squad of armed soldiers with their Arisaka rifles at port arms jogged to our house. Private Saito was among them. As they turned the street, his stomach must have turned inward as he realized who they were after: Tay.

We were already alerted. The dogs sensed their coming and barked. Without entering the house, the corporal in charge shouted in broken English and guttural accent from the front yard.

"Man in the house, come down!"

Tay stuck his head out the window in recognition of the order, quickly got dressed, and descended the stairs to join the detail. My aunts and my mother watched, concern on their faces as Tay was led away.

155

Esi and Mari were up early the next day to milk the mother goats before releasing them to pasture. Once done, Esi walked to the chicken coop to let the hens out in the yard to roam free. As she was about to release the latch, she espied a dripping ball of cloth just within the gate.

Her cry of alarm shattered the quiet morning as she recognized it. Tay, arriving home late the previous evening, had stripped the bloodied, tattered shirt off his back and stuffed it inside the chicken coop before tiptoeing up the stairs.

I sat up from the bed as if from a bad dream at the sound of her wailing. My father lay on his side of the bed facing away from me.

His hair was damp. There was a cut on the right side of his scalp that was congealed with blood. His left cheek was swollen, the right eyelid a mere slit.

On his elbows, back, and buttocks were deep, raw, angry red abrasions and gouges rife with embedded sand. The feet and ankles showed rope burns. There were deep blue bruises on both thighs. The bruises on his rib cage made it difficult for him to breath.

The bedroom was instantly filled with wails and sobs as everyone rushed in to look. Nay calmly took charge, sending us off to assigned tasks (mine was to find his slippers; to this day I question the relevance of such an order).

Nay opened a medical kit to minister to his wounds.

"I was the sixth man when I got there. Heral, Tonyo, Jose, Pedring, Ninoy were already rounded up. It did not look good," Tay spoke to explain.

All selected were sympathizers to the resistance.

"'Where is Captain Toribio?' The officer looked into the eyes of each man.

"'We do not know, sir.' we said individually and respectfully. When it was my turn, I looked down, daring not to look at his face, a gesture deemed to be insulting. The commandant came

156

so close as if he wanted to peer into my innermost thoughts. I smelled a fishy odor on his breath.

"Being an officer, he was armed with a sword by his side. I had hoped not to make him angry lest he draw his weapon and behead each of us.

"He barked out an order to his subordinates. The beatings began. We fell to the ground, then were kicked and beaten with rifle butts for several minutes. I managed to crouch to protect my belly. At a sharp command, the soldiers stopped.

"The officer had thought of a better idea at inflicting torture. We were all marched out of the compound, halting in front of the flowing artesian well."

Tay paused for a deep breath and tried to compose himself before continuing.

"Each man was made to lie on his back on the gravelly street. A square piece of muslin cloth was draped over our faces, feet trussed together, hands tied with rope on each side away from the body. We heard the sound of empty cans being filled with water from the flowing well."

Tay felt liquid being poured over his covered face. At first he thought they were being given water to drink, but the soldiers continued to dump water over the cloth masks. Now everyone struggled to breathe through the wet cloth, gagging, and trying to turn their faces away. Tay tried to free his hands from the restraints, but the booted feet of the soldiers standing on either side of him ground his hands and wrists against the gravelly road each time he moved to resist. He stuck out his tongue to tent the cloth mask away from his nostrils and tried to calm himself before he passed out.

In the darkness, amid the relay of soldiers taking turns at filling the water cans, Saito managed to assign himself to Tay. Hovering above the helpless figure of his friend, he poured cans of water over the covered gagging face as he was ordered, but when unobserved, spilled some of the water on the side of his face allowing Tay a second of respite.

When Tay regained consciousness, he saw the figure of a soldier removing the rope binding his feet and hands and the dripping cloth off his face.

The water torture was over.

"Sir," Tay moaned, speaking out first in behalf of his men. "I don't know where Toribio is, but I can take you to his house."

For speaking without permission, Tay was rewarded with a blunt blow with a rifle butt close to his left eye. He swiveled his eyes left and right. Everyone was badly hurt but alive as the intent of the tormentors was to extract information. It was now dark and well into the night.

Tay and the others were hauled to their feet flanked by a squad of soldiers. They marched in the night lit only by stars. Tay took the group on a shorter path to Toribio's hacienda through a few solitary houses, which was his intent. Dogs barked, challenging their trespass.

Tay knew this was good and he was right.

A kilometer beyond the barking dogs, he heard a thump, followed by another. It was the distinctive sound of a wooden pestle striking the side of a wooden mortar, a long piece of hollowed out log used to thresh rice grain from its stalk. Another distant sound from a mortar followed by another was heard faintly in the distance. It was meant to be a warning signal. Who would be pounding rice in the dead of night?

The sound would carry deep and far and would assuredly be enough to warn, not Toribio who was hiding up in the mountain, but Toribio's family, giving them ample time to escape.

Several kilometers later, they heard the rush of bubbling water at a creek, which had to be crossed by a flimsy foot bridge made from bamboo poles. It allowed one person at a time. Tay pointed to a house in silhouette across the water.

"That is Toribio's house."

The Japanese soldiers crossed in haste and surrounded the structure. Unannounced, the officer broke open the flimsy door.

No one was home, children, wife, and dogs included. They searched the granary, which was separately constructed, and overturned the wooden rice mortar dugout in the event that someone was hiding in it.

Grabbing the wooden pestles resting inside the dugout, they beat the rickety door of the granary off its hinges. Inside the dark room they inspected every nook, cranny, and looked up over the rafters.

Finding no one, they angrily kicked over and with rifle butts broke every single earthen amphora jar leaving spilled rice grain and molasses all over the floor.

It was now well past midnight. Though frustrated at coming up empty-handed, the Japanese officer felt a measure of satisfaction. He had done everything he could.

He had "saved face," very important in Oriental culture.

The tired group plodded back to town. It was almost dawn. No one said a word. They passed a house along the road close to town. Tay spoke to the commandant in halting Nippon, which caught the latter by surprise in that he could speak in his language.

"That is my house. Would you let me go? I am the school principal. I promise to be at the school tomorrow."

Perhaps realizing they had no provision for a stockade to detain prisoners, he did!

The rest were also released to their homes, grateful to be alive.

Recovery

Fearful the Japanese soldiers would check on him, Tay hobbled off to school the next day as promised. He tarried a bit longer at the front steps leading to his office so that he could be seen in full view by the Japanese sentry at the guardhouse fronting the garrison across the street.

At school recess, Nay came over, checked his dressings, and fed him a bowl of rice and corn gruel. His physical wounds healed over the next nine months.

There remained a residual buzzing in his left ear and occasional headaches on the same side where he had received a heavy blow close to his eye with a rifle butt. This was to continue to affect him throughout his lifetime.

He started growing vegetables in the garden and puttering about the yard. One night after dinner, he recounted his water torture and marveled at how well and fit he was feeling. In a jocular vein, he asked me, "Do you remember Heral, the man across town whose belly sticks out as if he has a pillow stuck beneath his front shirt?"

I nodded and waited with bated breath to see where this was leading.

"Well, Heral was not smart enough. When the Japanese soldiers poured cans full of water over his face, he drank every drop of it." He paused for effect. "And this is what happened to him."

He joined both hands and made an exaggerated arc that described Heral's belly, puffed up his cheeks, and brought down his chin, making his jowls seem bloated.

I laughed hard at the joke. Nay gave Tay a meaningful look, not amused.

We then knew that Tay was healthy again, both physically and mentally.

The Messenger

A man came to our home in pitch-black darkness, announced by the urgent barking of our dogs. Tay rose swiftly off the bed to retrieve his rifle secreted in a hollowed out wooden post of the *sala*.

Esi parted the nipa shingles on the outer wall of her bedroom and scanned the yard and front of the house. She saw a man's outline just outside the gate and determined he was alone.

Satisfied by Esi's report, which he trusted because of her uncanny night vision, Tay commanded the dogs to silence and invited the man to come up the stairs. With loaded rifle on the floor in easy reach, Tay bade the man sit in one of the rattan chairs on the covered balcony.

Tay did not know this man. He could not have been more than eighteen or twenty years of age. He appeared uneasy, snorting every now and then as if he had a problem unblocking his nostrils. "I come with a message from Captain Toribio," he began.

Tay's fingers clawed tightly against the arms of his chair, but he kept his composure and refused to take the bait before replying.

"Captain Toribio went to war and is presumed to have died along with every man from the town of Bisal who fought with him. Not one has returned."

He asked the man to leave. Japanese collaborators were everywhere.

The young man sat back eyeing Tay's rifle before he said, "The Captain anticipated that you would be skeptical."

He then mentioned two things that only Tay and Toribio shared: the time of day and place of their very first meeting by the spring well.

And the Goathole.

Tay was now completely convinced.

Decision Time

The day following the young man's visit, Tay and Nay spoke quietly in the bedroom in the falling dusk. The alleged message from Toribio required a decision that night.

Having given Nay the full narrative earlier in the day, there still were lingering doubts about the authenticity of the news. Was Toribio really alive? Was this a trap being set for him that could cost him his life?

Tay knew there was a risk, but he wanted Nay to know he had made up his mind to go. He owed Toribio, and he intended to pay him back.

They embraced in the dark. Nay's stifled sobs betrayed her fear that this might be their last night together.

Reunion

Careful not to awaken me, Tay tiptoed out of the bedroom. It was just past midnight. Already dressed before he went to bed, he went down the stairs into the darkness.

The dogs rose on their front legs eager to do their master's bidding. A gentle pat on their heads settled them down.

Tonight, he did not want to be seen by man or dog. He needed stealth, so he clung to the shadows and kept off the trail. He was on his way to rendezvous with his old and dear friend, Captain Toribio.

As he reached the top of the dike, he crouched and half loped so as not to expose his silhouette as a man, but more like an animal wandering around in the dark. Maintaining a southerly course, he came across a narrow white swath of a dirt path leading to the river.

This was the cutoff he was looking for, a white scar on the grassy dike made by the passage of countless feet stunting the growth of the underlying grass.

At the river's edge, he tarried in the darkness and cupped his hands to his pursed lips, blew a simulated hoot of an owl, paused a few seconds, and emitted two more hoots. A *banca* glided in the black water toward his hiding place.

Bolol, Toribio's vassal, gestured. As fast as Tay could find his seat, both men paddled silently toward the opposite bank. Another dark figure of a man was waiting.

Bolol whispered in Tay's ear. "This man, another guerilla, will lead you to Toribio."

The two men walked fast in the dark for several kilometers following a narrow path of white dirt leading up the mountain until they arrived at an incline flanked by two massive stone boulders. Another man in hiding came out fully armed, recognized them and let them through.

They walked for ten kilometers, came to a stand of trees surrounded by more boulders, and sat to drink thirstily from a canteen. They had been on the march for three hours. Dawn was breaking.

Tay realized he was in the midst of a concealed camp of armed men who were beginning to stir into wakefulness.

Most of the rifles appeared to have just come out of their cases, as were the shiny brass jacketed bullets showing through the cartridges that held them.

Were these Captain Toribio's guerillas?

His guess was affirmed by the familiar figure of his friend. The smile was unmistakable; he appeared gaunt, and he walked with a noticeable limp.

Each regarded the other like a man inspecting a water buffalo for sale, checking for any physical flaws. Toribio noticed the reddish welt of a scar on Tay's forehead from his ordeal at the hands of his tormentors. His eyes softened in an expression of sympathy.

Toribio led Tay by the arm out of earshot of the men toward a makeshift shelter behind some dense shrubbery that served as his command post. They sat on rough-hewn chairs on either side of a flat slab of rock used as a table.

In a recessed shelter against a rock wall sat a man with a headset utilizing a radio powered by a bicycle-operated dynamo pedaled manually by another guerilla.

"I am sorry that you had to be tortured on my account. We made the mistake of allowing a man who is not from our town to be one of us. He is the one who ratted out on me. We have since taken care of him," Toribio began.

"After I came to this place a year ago with Gonzalo, I sent him down to my hacienda. My vassals came up here to bring food supplies and build me a shelter. Word got around to other soldiers who had escaped the war in Bataan and Corregidor.

"Those who chose to have since joined up with us. We have been supplied with a radio, as you have seen, with which we communicate with other guerillas in this mountain and with American submarines offshore. We have been receiving caches of guns, supplies, ammunition, and explosives, and have hidden them.

"I want to acquaint you of your upcoming role in the months ahead."

Over the next hour, the two bent their heads close, talking quietly, like a priest listening to a penitent at a confessional. "You are our closest operative in town to the enemy. Use your eyes and ears. Report to us anything of significance. Do not confront them."

Toribio paused, then added, "At a future date, you will be visited by someone. We know him only as *Duron,* the locust. If he is the right man, he will ask about wild-boar hunting. Your reply is that it was great in the week of July 29. You are to bring him to me."

Tay's pulse quickened. These were orders fraught with dangerous implications that would raise the risk in regard to his safety and that of his family.

Toribio winked at Tay and stood up. The meeting was over. Just above head level he parted a canvas flap exposing a ledge out of which he pulled out two army rations of corned beef hash. They ate it cold, wordlessly, spooning every morsel hungrily into their mouths.

Finally satiated, Toribio took a crumpled pack of Lucky Strikes and a book of matches out of his breast pocket.

"Smoke as many as you like, but do not take anything back with you."

Tay stared at the spiral of smoke as he blew it out of his nostrils, luxuriating in the tobacco's aroma. He had one burning curiosity.

"I know this part of the mountain and have hunted here with you over the years. I am not aware of a place where you could possibly hide such a sizeable cache of weapons as you have just described."

His friend rubbed at his aching hip, snuffed out the smoldering butt of his cigarette on the ground with the toe of his shoe, reflected for a second, and told him.

"Before the war began, fishermen plying the river had long noticed some water trickling out of the sloping ground between the river's edge and the earthen dike. Low shrubbery had grown around the now-hidden opening.

"A very large reptile with a girth as wide across as a pillow supposedly lives in it. Nobody had seen the rest of this reptile but from the description of its girth, such a snake would be at least twenty feet long and able to devour a large animal or even a man. So it was a place that was never trodden even by the most curious."

The Monitor Lizard

The US submarine surfaced at night off the coast of Lingayen Gulf in the seacoast town of Bani. Waiting at the rendezvous point were Filipino guerillas in three large *bancas* with outrigger motors.

The cargo of guns and ammunition were offloaded swiftly. Two Americans in civilian clothing left the submarine, then climbed in the *bancas* with the guerillas before the sub dove back to the safety of deep water.

Sergeants Henry Maddox and John Paine of the US Marines were part of a clandestine group of operatives tasked to support the guerilla efforts in the area.

A radio communication network had been set up throughout the island. Their next assignment was to find ways to expedite the anticipated flow of war material from sea to land, to supply a future counteroffensive against the Japanese.

In previous conversations with the guerillas, the snake lair was casually mentioned, and the two men were ordered to investigate.

That evening they were taken to the riverbank, then traveled on foot until they heard the silent trickle of water they followed to the opening. They were to be picked up in twenty-four hours.

As the veil of grass was parted, both men saw an opening roughly the size of a man's head in the sloping ground. They were dismayed, having expected to see a cave with a yawning mouth.

The men pulled trench shovels from their backpacks and began digging at the soft clay. What did they have to lose? They weren't going to be picked up for the next twenty-four hours, so they had time to explore.

Paine stuck his hand all the way to his elbow through the draining water and upward into a void. He felt a draft of cold air through his fingers, suggesting an open space. Their expectations rose.

Both men attacked to enlarge the opening with renewed vigor, not stopping until they could poke a head and eventually a shoulder into the opening within. A lit flashlight was shoved inside.

There was a shallow puddle of water on the floor about eight feet across. Both men now fought to be the first to see farther. Maddox, the skinnier and more agile of the two, prevailed.

He looked upward into darkness, which was pierced by the shaft of illumination of the flashlight.

He half shouted, "Holy crap, Henry. You have to see this!"

Paine, disappointed that he had to wait his turn, needed no further prompting. Grabbing Maddox by his trousers, he yanked him bodily from the hole like a cork being pulled out of a champagne bottle, and peered inside to see for himself.

Geologists call it a lava tube, a roughly cylindrical cavern coated from floor to ceiling with what looked like dried coal tar. It was huge. The jagged margins of the lateral walls, ceiling, and floor indicated where the lapping waves of massing molten lava from an underground volcano had slushed around, cooled off, and jelled sixty thousand years ago when the islands of the Philippines rose from the sea, leaving in place a permanent non-collapsed tube leading downward all the way to the river where it expended its energy.

It had floored depressions here and there where shallow puddles of water accumulated when it rained and flooded. There were ledges and cul-de-sacs. Crawling inside the cavern, they were able to stand, their faces and exposed forearms immediately brushing against giant spider webs that reached from floor to ceiling.

A deep hiss—like air being forced through bellows in a blacksmith's shop—suddenly echoed through the cavernous tunnel. The two men pointed their flashlights in that direction. Two pinpoints of light winked back at them, followed by a cracking sound that broke the stillness.

Paine felt a sharp slap on the side of his bare head, tearing off part of his now-bleeding right ear. The impact sent him reeling sideways, landing with a splash on his side in the shallow puddle of water in front of them. The hiss was heard again, more urgent. Maddox, taken by surprise, stepped back and was spared from being lashed.

The monitor lizard was on a recessed shelf where it guarded a nest surrounded by the remains of a dead chicken. It was protecting two offspring that made high-pitched hisses in a poor imitation of their mother, sounding more like the sibilant wheeze from the chest of a man in an asthmatic attack.

The adult lizard was about five feet in length from snout to a muscular tail that tapered like a flexible whip. By its size, one well-placed lash could break a man's forearm.

It had the appearance of a gecko lizard only many times larger and more menacing. The grayish-black body was smooth and slick, the snout flat, the nostrils close to its mouth. The open jaws dripped with saliva laden with poisonous bacteria, and revealed a set of sharp upper and lower teeth meant to sink deeply, holding onto its prey for as long as it wished.

The reptile hyperextended its forelegs and displayed four-inch-long, curved, pointed claws. Its fully expanded lungs broadened its chest to the approximate width of a pillow, as rumored. It had overcome the odds, had grown very large, formidable, and deadly, having now become an apex predator.

The lizard did not leave the ledge because of its offspring and seemed to regard these two intruders with malevolence. It angled its body as if to move away.

171

Actually, it was assuming the striking position, its tail poised to lash out with maximum force like a whip in a stagecoach driver's hand.

The sudden splashing sound of water, caused by Paine attempting to get up from the shallow puddle and still unaware as to what hit him, confused the reptile. It launched its five-foot-long body in the direction of the perceived threat.

Paine barely managed to extend his flashlight when he felt the reptile's fully extended front claws rake his shirt into shreds. The teeth sunk into the source of the intruder's flashlight. Paine's forearm took the brunt of the lizard's forty-pound weight as he jerked his elbow in a protective reflex.

The reptile grunted as it took the impact of Paine's sharp elbow in its gut. It landed on all fours, yet maintained its firm bite on the flashlight, the beams bouncing off the walls and outlining part of its head.

Maddox unslung his carbine and prepared to fire but didn't, fearful of hitting his buddy. The decision what to do next came as a reflex reaction. As the reptile prepared to lash out with its tail again, it turned sideways. He raised the butt of his rifle overhead. Guided by the flashlight in the serpent's mouth, he found his mark.

The crunch on the top of the giant lizard's skull caused it to open its mouth and release the flashlight. Now it launched to attack with its open jaws, but apparently concussed, seemed disoriented in locating Maddox, the intended target.

The reptile's jaws snapped into nothingness. Its front legs failed to support it head as it dropped with a sickening thud on the sharp jagged points of the lava tube floor.

Maddox and Paine were ecstatic. Their discovery had solved a vital problem of storage and logistics. Let the lore persist about the large snake and its lair. It would deter curiosity and prying eyes and work to their advantage in regard to what they intended to do with their discovery.

Toribio and Tay shook hands. In parting, Toribio said, "Stay alert and be careful, my friend. You are safe until you get to the foot of the mountain. My men will see to it."

Tay gathered his belongings. He had taken a few steps when the Captain caught up with him and whispered, "I almost forgot since you did not ask. The snake lair, which we now know was the home of a large monitor lizard, leads to your backyard. Its upper end starts at the Goathole."

Descent from the Mountain

Tay followed the dirt trail down the mountain. He was in better spirits, his feeling of guilt assuaged knowing that Captain Toribio was very much alive. He noticed that dark clouds blocked the sun; the wind suddenly came in sporadic gusts. Hearing thunderclaps, he quickened his pace as lightning streaked close by, striking a tree.

The rain came, changing the dirt trail into wet slippery clay. He headed for a stand of trees and found a hollowed-out live tree trunk that looked safe and dry. By then it was almost dark. He decided to stay where he was and wait for daybreak.

A few kilometers down the mountain trail, there was a crossroad. One footpath led toward the riverbank, the other parallel and toward the mountain. Six horsemen were stopped in earnest conversation in a rough circle. A water buffalo on a tether, its back loaded with bundles, waited docilely behind. It was probably taken forcibly from a hapless farmer and his family in return for sparing their lives.

They were *tulisans,* roving bands of bandits hiding in the mountains who preyed on the helpless and those living in isolation. The bandits were all armed with rifles. A *bolo* lay on a scabbard at each man's belt. Raindrops dripped freely down the tough, dried calabash half-gourds which served as water repellent hats; their raingear was made of overlapping layers of palmetto fronds gathered around the neck with twine. The fronds flared away from the shoulders to deflect the rain from the rest of the body like an open umbrella.

Two of the men had been having an ongoing argument all night. The rain and cold were not helping to allay their increasingly foul mood. Suddenly, one man, perhaps the leader, drew his *bolo* off his waist and lifted the weapon upward toward the man on his right. The intended victim saw the weapon too late and raised his hand to parry the anticipated blow.

The attacker changed the trajectory into a horizontal slash across the man's unprotected torso. The sharp blade struck the soft web belt between the clips of ammunition on the bandolier across the man's belly. Blood and entrails spilled onto the man's lap.

He knew he was mortally hurt and dug at his horse's flank to get away.

The assailant replaced his weapon on its sheath. No one seemed concerned about pursuit of the fleeing man. His wound was grave and he would probably die. Their share of the night's booty would be shared among five men, no longer six.

Tay crawled from his shelter at daybreak in the foggy silence of the forest, not knowing how lucky he was at not having ventured farther down the trail the night before. He retrieved his *bolo,* which he had kept at the ready during the night, and started down the mountain.

He first heard it, the buzz of a thousand fluttering wings, like bees converging on an intruder attacking their beehive. It was directly ahead of him.

The smell of human waste assailed his nostrils as he approached a bend in the trail. Bottlenose flies, two to three times the size of a housefly, their distended bellies iridescent blue with yellowish-green highlights reflecting in the early sun's rays, were feasting on the fluid that spilled from the torn entrails and various parts of the dead *tulisan.*

Tay was in near panic. He side-stepped the dead body, covered his mouth and nose with one hand, and tried not to look. As soon as he was past, his feet took off with a fleetness he knew he could not muster in an ordinary footrace. His heartbeats drummed loudly in his chest.

Gasping for air, he finally had to stop. He knew his rubbery legs would buckle if he sat, so he leaned against a tree, head bent down. Sweat flowed freely down his face, chin, and the tip of his nose.

After what seemed like hours, he became calm and composed. Logical reasoning took over as he made an assessment. First, he was lucky to be alive. Second, he was well hidden. Third, he had to get off the mountain safely and expeditiously, because what he had just seen was the unmistakable body of a bandit who had suffered a violent end.

Who knows? Maybe they were hiding close by!

He scanned the area, espying movement a hundred meters away. It was light beige against green foliage, not a man but a horse, grazing, its head bobbing up and down. It appeared to be on a tether.

Unsure if there was anyone else around, he waited for another hour.

The sun was already past noon when he made his move to approach. The horse was snagged to vine and tall grass by a trailing rope. Part of the saddle and its coat and mane were caked in drying blood.

Tay assumed that the horse belonged to the dead man. He set the reins, cut off the trailing rope, and after overcoming the queasiness in his gut, he quickly mounted the saddle slimy with blood.

Two hours later, he arrived at the river bank still feeling exposed and vulnerable. He rode the horse into a fast gallop on the level trail heading in the direction of the embankment, urging his mount to plunge into the river ten feet below.

Horse and rider were swept by the current, managing to crab their way five hundred meters downriver to the safety of the opposite bank.

Stranger on a Horse

I was standing outside on the *batalan*, the open porch at the back of a traditional Filipino home. Next to me sitting on her haunches washing pots and preparing supper was Aunt Mari.

Silhouetted against the sunset, I saw a man on horseback across the pond where a dirt path led from the dike.

He waved. I was unsure if I knew him, but I waved back. As he got closer, I recognized him.

It was Tay, my father. Mari and I yelled excitedly, bringing everyone else to the *batalan*. We were all curious. Where did the horse and the unfamiliar native raingear come from?

Tay dismounted to unsaddle the horse by the pond, where the animal helped itself to a long, cool drink. Nay went down the stairs, shawl around her shoulders, nodding an imperious silent command for us to stay put.

Tay was scrubbing dried blood off the horse's flanks with dried grass plucked from the ground when Nay reached him. They conversed quietly.

Nothing more was said after that. The horse, a beige stallion with white mane and tail, was taken to the pond early each morning, given a drink, bathed and brushed, then tethered on a long rope to graze on the grassy slopes of the dike.

Clandestine Visits (1943)

Voices in a strange language came from the covered balcony as if in a dream. I reached with one hand to Tay's side of the bed, only to find he was not there. I perceived a faint sliver of light from the oil lamp piercing a parting of the thin palm shingles that made the wall separating the balcony from my bedroom.

I walked toward the sound of conversation and saw two men I had never seen before. One was tall with a shock of fair hair. His knees were drawn up above his seat in the rocking chair. He cast a faint smile in my direction as I came to stand by Tay's chair.

Another man, slightly on the lean side and the shorter of the two, sat on the sofa across from Tay. His eyes kept looking outward past the stairs in the direction of the narrow lane that passed by the house as if wary of unseen company.

Upon seeing me, he grabbed his rifle resting next to him on the sofa and laid it on the floor as if trying to hide it from my line of sight.

Both had long noses, pale skin, and ruddy faces. They were dressed incongruously in drab peasant clothes, which did not mask their appearance as different from a native Filipino. They were each armed with a rifle and a sidearm holstered at the waist within easy reach.

On the table in front of Tay was a revolver that looked like those worn by actors in a cowboy movie. A short-barreled gun with a long cartridge lay in an open brown box. I learned later that it was a submachine gun with a collapsible stock. They were brought in by these men for Tay's personal use. In the flicker of the oil lamp, I could see Tay's pleasure as he examined the weapons.

In addition to the old reliable Springfield rifle, which he had kept hidden in a false hollowed-out post just behind the door, Tay would now have three weapons around the house.

Sergeants Maddox and Paine were talking quietly under the roofed balcony. Tay listened carefully.

"Guavas are ripe."

Tay waited for Paine to say more, but none came. It was a coded message meant for Basilio, a man from across town. Tay was the messenger who was to convey it. If caught by the Japanese, Tay could be forced to repeat the message but could not divulge its meaning.

Nay had been cooking a hot meal and called from the dining room. The two men rose and ate quickly before melting back into the obscurity of the darkness outside.

The men and a group of guerillas had come that night with more war supplies but had misjudged the amount of storage space left at the Goathole—there was almost a *banca* full left to stow away with no place to hide the supplies.

The guerillas and Sergeants Maddox and Paine, gravely concerned about their safety, did not wish to tarry another minute, so they departed. Tay was left with the unconcealed weapons and needed to figure what to do with them.

Tay had agreed to the suggestion, a perilous temporary option, of storing the overflow under our stilted house. They covered the pile with hay, brush, and sticks. That same night, after Paine and Maddox were gone, Tay went out in the night. Following the riverbank he took a circuitous way on foot to the other side of town to find Basilio, who would figure out what to do.

Tay was in bed by daybreak and glad it was Saturday. He did not have to report for work at the school the following day.

Basilio, the smuggler, came to our yard the following night. With him were two dozen men with animal-drawn sleds. Tay was already downstairs and had tied up Betty and the rest of the dogs, muzzling their faces to stifle any barking.

In methodical fashion as if pre-rehearsed, each man took to his assignment—loading the crates of guns, ammunition, and military supplies beneath the house onto the waiting sleds.

In less than an hour they were gone, the wooden skids of the sleds slithering noiselessly out the back way along grassy trails.

Basilio tried to think ahead. Something had to come up. He was running out of room and ideas where to stash additional supplies.

The Visit

The *calesin*, a two-wheeled open carriage drawn by a fine horse, pulled up in our front yard in the lengthening shadows of twilight. At the reins was a man I had never seen before but had heard so much about—Uncle Tirso and wife Violeta, the sister of my Tay, Mari, and Esi.

It had been a long journey. Both had traveled all day from one of the inland towns. Tirso's heavily pomaded black hair looked grayish with dust, agitated by the horse and carriage from the dirt road.

Both were dressed in resplendent clothes. Tirso's face seemed burnt from hours of traveling under the sun; or was that the flush of skin from a nip or so of alcohol during the trip?

Violeta stepped down to the unbounded delight of Mari and Esi at this unexpected reunion with their older sister. Dida held Noli, my infant baby brother, in her arms as Nora beamed happily in the background.

Even the dogs brushed their wagging tails against the sisters' legs as if begging to be part of the happy celebration.

The raucous conversation was interrupted by a deep throated whinny from the direction of Tirso's stallion. A similar response came from the backyard.

Tirso was immediately in quiz mode. "Do you have a horse?"

Tay nodded quietly but declined to elaborate. Knowing Tirso, among other things, he would want to inspect every inch of the horse's mouth, withers, pastern, and fetlock in a manner that would shame a veterinarian. There was just enough daylight left for him to free his horse from its harness, give it food and water, and bed it down for the night.

Both men agreed to wait to check the horse until morning. They repaired to sit on the covered balcony at the top of the stairs while the women cooked and gossiped.

Tay lit the oil lamp and produced a gourd of *basi* and two drinking cups from beneath the low table that separated them.

Between sips, they exchanged pleasantries about family, the local news, and the impact of the war in their lives.

After the first cup of wine, Tirso became a changed man, He reached for the wine gourd without waiting for his host, Tay, to refill his glass.

A half hour into his third cup, Tirso could no longer contain himself. He asked the question that had been searing his brain.

"Where did you get your horse?" He must have asked himself how Tay, a man of little means as compared to him, could afford to own one.

Tay had been thinking of what to say since Tirso had asked the question earlier. Now he was ready.

"I did not buy the horse. Nor did I steal it."

He paused to pour more wine in Tirso's cup before adding, "I found it astray on the other side of the river a few kilometers from here. There was a saddle on its back and I did not see anyone. It was a territory of dangerous roaming bandits, so I rode on the horse to get away as fast as I could."

The women called for the men to come inside for supper. Reaching for the oil lamp, Tay stood up, smiling.

"You will get a chance to look the stallion over in the morning before we take our horses out to pasture. After that, if you'd like, we could go and watch the cockfights at the arena nearby."

Tirso and his Family

Tirso was an alcoholic, congenial when sober, garrulous when inebriated. On the latter occasions, he was wont to beat his wife using fist, cane, or the *latigo*, the horse whip, on a whim or at the slightest provocation.

He was a Master of *Arnis*, the Filipino martial art of stick fighting. As I grew up, I overheard conversation from the town elders that he was someone you wouldn't want to physically confront.

Tirso's father, Don Bernardo, was raised as a gentleman. His father was a Spaniard who married the daughter of a *datu*, the uppermost class of the Filipino caste system in the pre-colonial days. Don Bernardo owned wide tracts of land and had vassals working for them in and around his villa and lands.

The Don also raised fighting cocks with aggressive pedigrees. Several dozen were taken out of their individual cages each day and tied on one leg with a string to a peg apart from each other to prevent one from jousting with the other. They were preened and groomed by personal handlers who made them spar against one another.

The entire day was filled with cock crows from this testosterone-filled stable.

In other parts of the province, additional stables of fighting cocks were being trained. The goal of all of this was to train them to become killers against other fighting cocks.

At some point, they would be called upon to sacrifice their lives in some dirt arena surrounded by hordes of lusty men on bleacher seats, who egged on their favored bird, armed on either or both legs with the *tari*, three-inch razor-sharp steel blades, for a few seconds of mortal combat and a chance for bettors to win or lose some money.

The appropriate occasions for the cockfights were timed to when people congregated for town fiestas or religious holidays.

16-Cockfight

Don Bernardo loved to dress up in his Sunday best for church, favoring white cotton pants that had been freshly ironed and stiff with starch to accent the creases. As he walked with cane in hand, people would acknowledge him with a nod, making way for him in deference to his high social status.

In public, Tirso's parents appeared like the model couple, one to emulate.

At home, things were different. The Don was quick tempered, more so after imbibing *basi*, the sugar wine that was always in adequate supply. He would slap his wife and beat her at the slightest whim or perceived provocation.

Tirso and his younger brother, Dolfo, passed through a similar gauntlet of punishment for reasons they did not always comprehend.

From the time they were four or five years of age, a whimper, not deemed appropriate for a male, within earshot of Don Bernardo was disciplined with a light cuff to the side of the head.

Improper eating manners, failure to rise when someone older came into a room, not doffing one's hat when inside a building, were likewise severely reprimanded.

As each child grew up, cane beatings were given expertly so that an outsider would not be able to detect the bruises.

Things were not always that bad. When sober, and especially after coming home from church, having repented to his confessor about his transgressions, he was generally expansive and in good spirits.

On Saturdays, he would walk outside to the courtyard where a table was set up. Atop were sticks—dried wooden canes whittled out of hard wood and further hardened by holding them over a hot flame.

These were the fighting sticks for the martial arts called *Arnis*. They were as short as a foot and as long as three feet. Others were six feet long; some were forked at one end or both.

The boys were summoned, whether they liked it or not. They learned the rudiments and later the fineries of combat and self-defense.

Don Bernardo was relentless and demanded perfection of each *kata* or movement. There were combat practices of man to man, two attackers against one defendant, and others.

The boys were not allowed to make any mistakes after a lesson was drilled into them. The penalty was harsh: bleeding face, cut ears, and lumps to the scalp, body, and extremities.

Dolfo was not enthused about the Saturday afternoon activity, but he never showed it.

Tirso, on the other hand, flourished and became more vicious as he grew. He almost beat to death one of the trainers, a man chosen from among the vassals, were it not from intervention of Don Bernardo. He was twelve years old then. His voice was getting husky.

On Sunday evenings, Don Bernardo retired early. The boys would sneak down the stairs under the house where earthen jars of rice wine and *basi,* sugar wine, and were fermenting. They helped themselves to a nip or two, snickering quietly between themselves at a joke in the dark.

When Tirso reached the age of fifteen, the boys had become regular visitors to the wine jars and thought nothing about having a cupful, then a pitcherful every Sunday night.

By that time Tirso had grown as tall as his father. He was also brawny from helping at the farm against the entreaties of the vassals who were afraid of the repercussions to their livelihood should the Don find out about it.

At suppertime one night, when Don Bernardo was served his jug of wine at the table, Tirso loudly asked the servant to bring him a cup and a jug of wine.

Dolfo almost choked on his buffalo jerky. Their mother's eyes stared in disbelief at Tirso. But as a woman, it was not her place. This was between a boy turned man and father. Confrontation was inevitable.

Don Bernardo, sitting at the head of the table, showed no emotion. He did not raise the ubiquitous cane that was always by his side. He nodded imperceptively for the manservant to follow Tirso's bidding.

The beatings stopped after that. Tirso's message was clear. Dolfo could not understand the change in Don Bernardo from that day onward.

When Tirso reached the age of sixteen, his mother, Dona Segunda, passed away. Two years later, Don Bernardo's eyesight began to fail. Not wanting to miss the adulation he received when he walked the streets, he continued to attend Sunday mass, usually accompanied by his head servant.

One Sunday he asked Tirso and Dolfo to accompany him instead. Dressed in an elegant *barong* shirt, a sparkling white pair of stiffly-starched white cotton drill pants, and spotless white shoes, he cut an imposing figure as he stepped outside the house gate.

It was a nice day for walking. Although he could not see, the breeze felt cool on his cheeks, and with the weather balmy, he could have imagined the sun shining with a few lazy white billows of clouds overhead.

Unbeknownst to him, it had rained heavily during the night. There were puddles on the dirt road in depressions made by the ruts of *carretela* wheels and horse and water buffalo hooves as they pulled farm carts laden with produce.

With one strapping boy on each side, he walked proudly basking in the attention he received from churchgoers who greeted him as befitted his social status.

Tirso had something else on his mind that day—a mild revenge for all the atrocities, real or perceived, he had endured from this old man, his father.

Ahead of them lay a rather large pothole in the middle of the road. When horses piss, they can urinate on the fly or plop round, greenish balls whenever and wherever they want.

Not so with the water buffalo. When this animal has to go, it has to make a full stop to make an all-out plop or take a full piss rooted in the same spot. No amount of lashing at its back would move such a beast until the business was done.

At the far edge of the mud puddle was a big mound of buffalo plop, its circumference requiring both arms linked to encircle it. It was possible to jump over the mud and land without calamitous consequences, but the margin for error was extremely slim.

Tirso warned Don Bernardo there were puddles about, which was true. His father nodded in understanding, trusting in his sons to navigate him safely.

"We will walk you close to the puddle's edge. Wait for my signal for you to jump. And don't worry. We will be on each side of you just in case you lose your balance."

Dolfo was mortified as he guessed what was about to happen. He wanted to utter a warning to the Don, yet he faltered; his mouth was open, but his voice box froze. He could only watch with terror in his eyes. Beads of sweat formed on his forehead and the top of his nose.

The countdown began.

Don Bernardo's form was a perfect "10." Knees bent slightly, body leaning forward, at the command "Jump!" from Tirso, he took off.

His feet landed in the middle of fresh warm buffalo plop, white shoes displacing a corona of gook that splattered in all directions of the compass.

Don Bernardo's white pants were speckled to mid-calf as if he were wearing a new fashion style of leggings.

Tirso never returned to his father's home. Instead, he moved farther away on the vast family property where the vassals built him a home.

Duron

Tirso and Tay were already in the yard at sunrise the next day. Tirso appeared unusually cheerful with no sign of a hangover from the previous evening of libation. Like a good horseman, he immediately tended to his horse.

Tay approached with Kerlat, our stallion, leading him on a coil of tethering rope, and the two men chatted away as they led the horses to the pond's edge. When the horses bent their heads to drink, Tirso ran his hands along Kerlat's flanks and quarters. Then he casually changed the subject. "How is the boar hunting this year?"

Tay's back stiffened at this unexpected question. His mind flashed back to the night of the beatings by the Japanese soldiers and the water torture. He became immediately wary of this man.

Only his eyes shifted.

It is not possible. His brother-in-law? Tirso continued to stroke the horse's mane.

Tay saw something he had never noticed before: an inch-sized tattoo on Tirso's inner right arm, obviously a recent one.

There it was, the unmistakable drawing of a locust. *Duron!*

Tay cleared his throat. He had no choice but to give the appropriate response.

"It was better last year, July 29, to be exact."

That afternoon, Tirso and Tay saddled their horses and headed toward the hills. They followed the spine of the earthen dike south, talking like two friends on unhurried business out for a late trot.

They waved at fishermen casting nets on their already fish-laden boats so as not to arouse any suspicion. Two hours later, they left the dike to find the dirt trail leading to Captain Toribio's hacienda.

Bolol waved to Tay in recognition as they approached.

Tay came home alone that night. Tirso was now in Bolol's hands and would be further vetted before he could meet Toribio face to face.

Or maybe not. If he said the wrong things to Bolol and his co-vassals, Tirso might never be seen again.

Tirso, the locust, turned out to be the real deal. Once he was alone with Toribio, he produced a rolled scroll secreted in the leather handle of his horse whip. It mapped the safe trails inland beyond Bisal, along which war supplies could be stashed.

These trails were used by Basilio in the months that followed, greatly alleviating the constant bottleneck of supplies brought in from the sea by American submarines and in hiding places along the riverbank.

Along rugged terrain where there were no trails, they used a relay of sleds drawn by water buffalo on flat-based wood runners. Once on level ground far from the town, a waiting group of wheeled carts continued the journey that could cover ground faster, albeit a little noisier; hooded lanterns under the lead cart barely illuminated their way.

Before daybreak, all activity ceased. Each man was back in his home to avoid the scrutiny of the Japanese soldiers or enemy collaborators.

Tirso was energized in his newfound role. He tried to be constantly involved with Basilio and his men in their night activities.

Tirso dared the traitor who would give him away. For protection, he armed himself with a nickel-plated revolver and a web of bullets around his waist. For insurance, he had his wife sew an extra sheath of cloth on the outside of his riding pants for his *arnis* sticks.

He urged Basilio to do the same. Basilio demurred, preferring to look like an ordinary farmer with a *bolo* on a wood scabbard at his waist. All seemed well.

Until one day…

Basilio's Notch

It happened at *Amesay Pare*, "where the priests bathed," a table-flat rock on the river bank, so named by the local people because it was where the early Spanish missionaries coming from the river by boat on a hot, blistering summer day had paused to cool off. They divested their cassocks to take a refreshing dip in the inviting clear water.

It had been an arduous journey. Basilio's party of six carts and twenty men had just finished a night-run delivery up the back trail to the next relay of men.

Eager to return to their homes, they retraced their tracks.

Basilio was the last to splinter away from the rest of the group.

Drenched in sweat, he arrived at the riverbank. The overheated water buffalo recognized where it was and quickened its pace, no longer responsive to the restraining tug. Basilio sighed and let it go.

At the water's edge he untied the cart yoke allowing the ungainly beast to plunge into the water snorting jets of water off its nostrils as it came up for air.

Basilio laid his clothes on the flat rock, floated on his back, and gazed at the starry sky.

He heard the click of pebbles. Two armed men, *tulisans*, were on the shore. One man dismounted, rifle drawn, and headed for the empty cart. The other remained on his horse, keeping a sharp lookout.

Basilio sank down in the water, keeping his profile low, eyes just above the surface. He regretted his stupidity in leaving his weapon, the *bolo,* next to his shirt, beyond his reach. The lookout silently pointed to the dark blot on the rock. Rifle at the ready, the bandit approached, picked up the *bolo* with the other hand, and peered cautiously over the rock edge.

Basilio saw the man staring at him. He knew the odds were against him, but he rose and took action. He grabbed the man by one ankle and pulled him into the water with all his might.

The surprised *tulisan* leaned back, supported by his back foot. His head struck the rock ledge with a sound like a breaking earthen pot thrown against the ground. The bandit's trigger finger tightened, discharging a harmless shot.

The head injury knocked the man unconscious, allowing the rifle to sink to the river bottom.

Basilio saw his chance and moved to wade back to shore. He was prepared to surrender himself to the second horseman rather than die by drowning.

He need not have worried.

The report from the gun firing off in the still evening and visions of a Japanese patrol running to investigate panicked the lookout. He dug at his horse's flank and fled, pulling the other man's horse along with him.

Still in knee-deep water, Basilio had a premonition and looked back. The man he had presumed dead had sneaked up and was only a couple of yards behind him. He redoubled his efforts to flee.

He slipped on mossy rocks and fell forward on outstretched hand. The man had caught up, his *bolo* poised to strike. Basilio groped desperately for a weapon and found a fist sized rock.

The assailant, fueled by a mad desire to exact revenge, lunged and lost his balance.

Seeing the strike coming, Basilio raised his hands out of the water to fend off the blow, but it was too late. The *bolo* came down, striking the outer side of Basilio's right leg just below the knee.

But there was an unintended consequence in his favor— in his closed fist was the rock that struck the man squarely in the temple as he stumbled, a mortal blow where the bony skull covering of the brain is at its thinnest.

Basilio lay gasping as he pushed the prostrate body off his chest. He saw the dark pools of blood, his own and that of the dead man. He looked down at his injured leg and saw a gaping wound as if a woodman's ax had made a notch on the trunk of a tree. It had severed all the muscles down to the bone.

To his surprise, he could stand and support his weight, a good sign that his leg bones were intact. He retrieved his clothes and used his shirt and belt to put a pressure dressing on his wound. He swayed and knew that if he fell, he would never muster the strength to get up again.

In his line of sight, he saw the rope tether lying close to his feet with the water buffalo still in the water. Bending down, he tugged at the rope until the beast obeyed and came to stand next to him.

Somehow, he was able to drape himself over the buffalo's broad back, turned it onto the trail leading for home, and tried with much effort not to pass out. It was now up to the animal to find its way home if Basilio were to survive.

Emilia, Basilio's wife, peered through the slit in the window next to her bed just in time to see Basilio slide off the buffalo's back in a heap. The barking of their dogs simmered to a soft whimper as they licked their master's face when they recognized him.

Emilia roused their two boys who slept side by side on a straw mat. They carried their father inside. The two girls asleep in one corner close to the kitchen door were awakened by the commotion and began to panic. Emilia silenced them and ordered them to boil water and get clean rags. They were aghast when they saw the extent of their father's injury.

The pain from their poking ministrations to dress the wound revived Basilio, who asked for a drink of water before focusing on the next priority.

Finally, he said to his sons, "Take me to the hills tonight. Send for the herb doctor to tend to me once I get there."

He told them about the dead *tulisan*, which alarmed the girls even more. "Have one of the girls go to Don Sixto's house tonight and tell him about the dead body. He will know what to do." Then he passed out.

The two strapping boys, hardened by years of manual labor in the sugar and rice fields hefting heavy sacks of rice grain on their backs during the harvest season, took turns carrying their father in piggyback fashion at a fast dogtrot.

At the foot of the hills they espied outlined hazily in the distance a small hut belonging to a woodcutter they knew. They rejected the idea of asking for the man's help, recalling their father's succinct order: only the family and Don Sixto were to know.

The boys climbed up the increasingly steep hills; barely able to travel a dozen feet at a time without resting, each boy now held up Basilio on either side.

Nearing the top they saw another familiar landmark—a hidden ledge leading to a small cave: Basilio's hideaway, a rest stop on his smuggling forays.

Don Sixto was ostensibly a merchant who bought and sold rice and corn. At harvest time when the rice and corn had been duly apportioned in shares between the landowner and the workers of the land, Sixto came by and negotiated to buy what the farmers would not need. Usually the farmer had precious little to spare.

The landowner owned a large tract or even several tracts of land. The harvest was apportioned thus: half to the landowner, half to the farmer. That was generous. Some arrangements were 60 percent to the landowner, 40 percent to the farmer.

An outsider would say the arrangement of harvest distribution was slanted in favor of the landowner, who did nothing but own the land that his forebears seized from passive peasants who did not wish to resist even if they could, such being the way of the people to be non-confrontational.

The landowner, on the other hand, would contend that in return he allowed them to live on his land, raise poultry, pigs, and goats, and till the land around their homes for vegetables. Of course, a little of the produce from such endeavors must be shared with the landowner, such as eggs, chickens, and pigs for their meat.

Sixto gradually morphed to being called a Don by virtue of his growing wealth and influence, not by pedigree. His wide-open demeanor radiated trust, which generated more clients.

People with better means approached him as a go-between for a host of things, such as arranging marriages and mediating solutions between opposite factions to soothe fraying relationships.

Sixto also had a dark side. He had developed a friendly business arrangement with Basilio in the black market and the smuggling side of things.

On the night when Basilio's daughter slithered silently in the shadows of the trees lining the street leading to his house, Sixto was half asleep as though he had a portent of things to come.

He had awakened twice to empty his bladder in the chamber pot that the boy servant, sleeping on the floor outside his bedroom door to tend to his needs, had been summoned to empty, clean, and return.

The yard gate creaked open. The urgent whispered conversation between the servant who came to the door and Basilio's daughter brought Sixto to his feet and out the bedroom door in his nightwear.

The crying, heaving girl was ushered before his presence in the *sala*. Someone lit an oil lamp atop a desk. Sixto allowed her to speak in a torrent of words that he processed silently.

After a long pause, he spoke, "Go home. Tell no one about this, for the lives of all of us may be in danger."

With his warm open face gazing down at her, Basilio's daughter felt a sense of relief. She bent down to genuflect and kissed the back of Don Sixto's hand. She did not know what else to do. The local priest was always greeted this way.

Don Sixto peeked outside: not quite daybreak yet. There was little time left if he was to take advantage of the cloak of darkness and so much to accomplish.

He summoned two male servants to saddle a horse. Its hooves were to be padded. The men knew the routine, for they had done this before to smuggle in things clandestinely: food and people who wanted to travel inconspicuously in and out of town for whatever reason.

And now he was as much involved in the secret smuggling activities in war material with Basilio, his dear friend, albeit in a more covert way.

It was an activity of daring like this, fraught with danger, that he craved more than any sum of money; yet when he was doing it, he vowed it would be his last.

What if he got caught? What would happen to him and his family and all those whose lives revolved around and depended on him?

He knew the biting answer lay in the core of his brain. He lacked the physical gifts to ride a horse well, not just a horse but a bucking, spirited steed that would try to fling him off its back; to box, wrestle, fence in the *arnis* style like his new-found friend Tirso could do.

Tonight, here lay his chance to use his natural-born gift: cunning and the gift to improvise.

198

One man in the lead, the two servants trailing behind, they left through the side door of the yard leading to a narrow back trail just wide enough to allow the horse through. They cut through a grove of trees, blending in shadow with the thick brush and foliage. As they neared the river, they moved faster. Here there was little need for stealth, the rush of current overpowering any other noise.

They came upon the slab of flat rock and saw the empty cart. Not far away, in the shallows, they waded to retrieve the corpse of the *tulisan* entangled in dead brush.

Working quickly, they rolled the dead body of the *tulisan* into a straw sleeping mat. They ignored the bloodied face with the staring eyes. They trussed the bundle with rope and hefted it onto the horse's rump behind Don Sixto, who rode on the saddle.

The horse, perturbed by the strange smell of its bloody passenger, whinnied in protest and tried to wiggle sideways and back.

Don Sixto urged the horse forward for about a kilometer along the bank until he found a suitable place to ford the river to the other side, grateful it was summer and the water level had receded. While he waited for the panting servants running from behind to catch up, he dismounted to remove the mufflers on the horse's hooves.

By first light, he had entered the forest where there were huge boulders.

He chose a place, pointing. "Start digging here."

It was almost perfect. There were no signs of human traffic; it was elevated and invisible from casual view. They cut tree saplings and sharpened one end, levering recalcitrant rock and dirt to create a deep hole. The body, still wrapped in the mat, was thrown in the hole, then covered with dirt, rock, dried leaves, and rotting tree parts.

Basilio miraculously survived, living in the mountain for over a year helped by his family who nursed him back to health. The muscles in the wound remained separated and scarred, leaving a deep indentation, a hideous "notch" that could hold a pack of cigarettes without falling off. He was able to walk under his own power without cane or crutch.

Returning to Bisal in late 1944, he was just in time to oversee the final transfer of military supplies out of the goathole following the withdrawal of the Japanese soldiers from the town.

Latigo (the Whip)

Almost a year had passed since Tirso had visited the town of Bisal with his beautiful wife, my Aunt Violeta. The couple had a rocky, unstable marriage punctuated by bouts of physical abuse by Tirso at unpredictable moments. Their having no children to dote on was probably contributory. Tirso's clandestine activities with the guerillas in the days of the Japanese occupation contained the bottled up inner conflicts within him to an extent sparing Violeta from further beatings.

Following the demise of Don Bernardo, being the older of the sibling brothers, Tirso was now in charge of the vast hacienda, which stretched for over thirty kilometers, equivalent to nearly the size of a small town today. At his dying bed, the Don beckoned his two boys to sit close to him. In his hand he produced a folded yellowed document with a pictorial map of land and forest that Tirso and Dolfo never knew existed. Some words were scrawled with a rough hand, written in *Malay*

In Don Bernardo's case, the land started at the foot of a mountain and ended at its peak. It was never developed or inhabited. It was owned by his great, great grandfather, a *datu* or *maginoo*.

The *datu* were members of the uppermost tier of Filipino society fiefdom in the old days before Spanish colonization, who held sway over vast tracts of land. Beneath the *datu* were the freemen who could acquire any job, buy any property, or even acquire slaves and pay taxes. Next down were the *maharlika,* or warriors. Their job was to serve under the *datu*, fight and defend the village, and provide and make their own weapons, but they paid no taxes.

Lower down was the *aliping namamahay* who were slaves of the *datu* but could own their own homes within the village or *barangay*. At the lowest tier of the social system was the *aliping saguigilid*. These were the people who could be sold as servants. These last two groups could buy themselves out of this tier level and even move up in the society scale. As a general rule, the *saguigilid* stood little chance of emerging out of the poverty and debt, which incidentally was foisted on them even though the debt belonged to their ancestors.

Tirso and Dolfo made a mental note, looked at each other from either side of the Don's bed, and shrugged. They had more than enough to satisfy their needs with the hacienda running the way it was. Tirso accepted the document on behalf of the two siblings and took no further action for the time being.

Over the years, circumstances changed. Dolfo became a man about town who accidentally impregnated a young lady of a rival *datu* clan. He refused to accept paternal responsibility and bad feelings simmered. The chastened maiden's father appealed to his patron *datu*, but the latter's options other than taking his village to war was limited.

For this was the year of the Japanese Occupation. A Japanese militaristic order had emerged, and they controlled every aspect of Philippine society, including its way of resolving problems. Discretely, the *datu* asked a man, who happened to be a Japanese collaborator, over to his villa and inquired how he might offer a resolution to his constituent's dilemma. The latter reported the incident to the Japanese commander of the local garrison, who took it to a much higher level of aggression than anticipated.

Dolfo was arrested, questioned about possible anti-Japanese tendencies, and tortured for hours with fist, truncheon, and body blows, before he was finally released. When Tirso visited his brother at his home, he felt sickened; a dark menacing cloud replaced his flushed angry face. He became immediately transformed, paradoxically, in the opposite way. Vengeance, he was sure, must come, but he must remain calm. He knew that what he would do would lead to consequences that he must be prepared to deal with.

That evening, he began executing his plan. Violeta must leave and go into hiding that very night. More servants, the *alipins,* wives of the farmers working at the haciends, were called in to expedite packing of belongings and provisions. Violeta and her entourage of twenty loaded carts pulled by twenty water buffalo were many kilometers out by daybreak. A few more days march led them to the base of the mountain owned by Tirso and Dolfo.

Tirso's plan was cold-blooded and deliberate. He assigned some of his men to shadow the Japanese informer's movements for several days. Then he struck.

On a cloudy night bereft of moonlight, Tirso stepped out of the dark in front of the surprised informer on his way home. A clump of bamboo choked each side of the footpath, leaving the informer no place to go but to retrace his steps. He proceeded to run but stumbled.

Tirso withdrew two fire-hardened *arnis* sticks, each two feet long. One was forked at one end, the other a cylindrical rod not much larger than a plastic drinking straw. He tattooed the retreating man with a staccato series of drumbeat hits to whichever part of the body was left unprotected by the man's flailing arms. In particular he aimed for the sternum, neck, and temples. As the man gasped in pain, Tirso deftly pinned him by the neck to the ground with the forked stick and in one fluid motion drove home the pointed end of the second *arnis* stick into the open mouth of the dying man.

It was a perfectly executed, difficult death move made by an *arnis* master of the highest degree. And it was a calling card for the man who had betrayed his brother to the cruel Japanese.

Tirso's men were waiting to ensure his safe escape. They traveled in the backwoods all night and throughout the next day to reach the safety of his mountain property. Violeta was waiting. An advance party had built a lean-to for them to stay by. A shielded fire glowed, where food was cooked and ready for them to eat.

Over the next few days, Tirso and the men explored the mountainside and built a suitable hiding place for the couple. They also made sure there was an escape route in the event of a siege.

News always travels fast. That much is proven over the years. Wild animals smell danger in the wind and take flight to safety before the danger comes upon them.

It was less than a week when Captain Toribio heard of the news by word of (spy) mouth. A dead man from Tirso's town was found face down against a spike of a bamboo stump that by outward appearance had obviously impaled him. The presumption of accidental death was seriously entertained, but the driven spike in the mouth, the torturing of Dolfo, and the disappearance of the Tirso family from his *hacienda* would probably have deserved further investigation in latter day crime scenes. In Toribio's line of thinking, it was not a mere coincidence,.

He had a hunch he kept to himself. A few weeks later after said news, scouts reported seeing a band of men as they reconnoitered beyond the next ridge of the mountain. Were they *tulisans* or a new band of guerillas? He decided to investigate. Taking ten men, including the two scouts who last saw suspicious movement, they set out.

Three hours later Toribio came across the lower base camp where Tirso had slept that first night. There a smoldering fire with a lazy wisp of smoke rose faintly in the air with cooking pots nearby. He glassed the area with his binoculars. The men he spotted did not appear armed, save for the sheathed *bolos* at their waists. Looking up the mountainside above the men, he caught a glimpse of a printed dress.

Toribio led his men into the clearing with shouldered rifles and extended arms to show that they were not hostile. He smiled at Tirso's vassals and introduced himself. "I know who you are: Tirso's men. I just saw Violeta through my binoculars up there." He swept his right hand up toward the mountain.

Appearing much relieved, they broke into smiles, removed their straw hats, clutched them in their hands, and bowed briefly in a show of respect.

"The *patron*," referring to Tirso, "is up the mountain with some of the men building a hide," said the head of the kitchen detail. Toribio was now fairly certain as to why Tirso was here.

By the campfire that night following the joyous reunion between Toribio, Tirso, and Violeta, whom he had met previously on the couple's visit to Bisal, they squatted side by side on the grass, their backs against the warm boulder to take off the evening chill.

Toribio said in jest, "Do you remember the first time we met with you bringing those trail maps leading to the hiding places to store all those guns and supplies?"

"I had my initial doubts and did not know if I could trust you. One of my men was ready to kill you at my signal. You turned out to be an invaluable asset, and your efforts to help us meet other guerillas near your sector are much appreciated."

Tirso's turn came to speak. He was in a predicament due to what happened with Dolfo, and now he was on the run from the Japanese.

Toribio's words were reassuring. "You have helped us before. It is now our turn to help you. But in addition, we need certain favors."

Before the end of the evening, both sides had reached a mutual agreement. Three days later, Toribio's men returned to

Tirso's camp with enough rifles and ammunition to arm all the men, and a radio and radioman to train one of Tirso's men with final parting orders: do not attack until orders are received from the Americans, and collect and radio all information on certain wavelengths of the radio at certain hours.

Tirso set up an antenna on the highest peak of his part of the mountain, which sent and received messages with more clarity, dependability, and a farther range than most radios on the island. On a good day, his radio signals could reach all the way to Australia.

To hide his identity, Tirso assumed a *nom de guerre*: *Latigo* (the Whip), a name he learned to like. It would be his call sign over the radio and in the field of battle for the duration of the war.

Kerlat (Lightning)

This story would be remiss were I to omit further mention of the horse, a package of unbridled energy always impatient to gallop away at full stride once saddled with the rider on board. For that reason, I thought it appropriate to name him *Kerlat,* which means "lightning."

He wasn't tall. His back rose no higher than the top of my father's head at 64 inches. A large keloid, probably a slash mark injury caused by a sharp weapon, ran diagonally across his left flank.

Scars at the angles of his mouth from hard reining of the bit in his mouth were evidence he was ridden by a harsh master who pursued a life fraught with violence.

The sight and smell of another horse disquieted him, causing a twitchy pricking of the ears fore and aft. He would paw the ground, snort, and reflexively unload a stream of urine. On many an occasion, he had broken his rope, so powerful was the primal urge inside of him to investigate a potentially willing mare.

Tay put up with the horse's quirks and warts and sexual proclivities because, after all, he owed his life to Kerlat. Each morning at dawn, Tay dutifully led the horse to the pond to be watered, bathed, and groomed before tethering him out to pasture.

Kerlat was most vulnerable in the mornings. He would slog along reluctantly behind Tay, head down, eyes barely open like a man with a hangover after a night of carousing.

Tay perceived such moments of apparent docility by the horse as an opportunity. He put me astride the stallion's bare back;

my fingers grasped his luxurious mane. I loved the ripple of his powerful muscles beneath me and the animal scent of his unwashed coat.

One morning I got bored with the same plodding gait and felt that a change was in order. A dried hanging twig dangled invitingly ahead of me, and I had an idea.

I snapped off a piece as I passed by, in the same motion striking a blow with it at Kerlat's flank. In my exuberance, I miscalculated. The tip of the twig stung his crown jewels.

The stallion raised both hind legs, kicked, and bolted forward with a protesting snort.

Kerlat's sudden forward acceleration caused me to lose my grip on his mane, and tossed me off his back and over his tail. I would have fallen to the ground had it not been for Tay, who held the stretched rope as long as he could in an attempt to control a thousand pounds of the enraged beast.

Fortuitously, I slid astride the rope and landed safely in Tay's arms. He let the horse go, and he galloped away for the hills.

Lying to my father, I said I was all right, not wanting to tell him of the embarrassing rope burn between my legs very close to a sensitive part of my anatomy.

In the twilight and carrying a lit lantern, we set off to retrieve Kerlat. Guessing correctly, we headed for a meadow where two tethered mares grazed, our horse in their midst.

The neck rope was intact; its free end had been cut, leaving a short piece trailing three feet behind Kerlat's rump.

Tay slowly approached; the horse, seemingly unaware, continued to graze.

Tay stooped to pick up the end of the rope. Kerlat was waiting. He lashed out with his right hind leg, then moved a few paces away.

Tay sat on the ground groaning for a minute before motioning me to approach with the lantern. He lowered his drawers.

I saw the reddish imprint of the horse's hoof on Tay's right inner thigh. He continued to examine himself carefully in the adjacent vicinity for signs of collateral damage most particularly in the area of his manhood like a chimpanzee checking for fleas.

A hail from a familiar voice came out of the dark. Tay saw the bemused face of one of his friends as he approached.

The owner of the two mares had come to collect his horses for the night. When he heard our story, he kept a straight face and tried to appear sympathetic. He helped Tay to his feet, satisfied he was not seriously hurt.

The man approached Kerlat, who, without objection, allowed the man to retrieve the trailing rope that he handed back to us.

A few days later, Tay rode Kerlat in the direction of Don Toribio's hacienda.

He left the horse, saddle, grooming brush, rope, and feeding bucket in the care of Bolol until the Don's return from hiding in the mountain.

Japanese Soldiers Leave Bisal

Saito sat, stolid, in the back of the moving truck in a convoy of vehicles leaving the garrison in Bisal with three hundred men in the middle of the night. His body was pressed in the side bench between fellow soldiers, who had received their marching orders at chow time. They talked in hushed conversations about the oncoming return of the American military, already expected to make a landing in the middle of the Philippine Islands at Leyte.

On the eve of their departure after packing his gear, Saito sought a moment to be alone. He ventured out behind the garrison area beyond the latrines. Kneeling on the ground, he folded his hands in his lap and closed his eyes in silent prayer. Then he reached into his breast pocket and withdrew a small cloth pouch pursed with string. In it was a small clamshell polished to a gloss from repeated rubbing. It contained a pinch of incense and a lock of his father's hair.

Drawing his bayonet, he cut a lock of his own hair, commingled it with the rest, bowed, and meditated before reverently striking a match to set the symbolic pile aflame. He followed the upward spiral of the wisp of smoke and spoke quietly, mentioning his father by name. It was a pact he had made with his family before leaving Japan, and now he was bidding him farewell.

They're gone! All over town, people peered out their windows, not believing the news heralded repeatedly by Arturo, the self-appointed town crier. The derided flag of Japan with the red sun was not at its place at the top of the flagpole in the center of town.

Captain Toribio was not unaware. His company of guerillas had been receiving coded radio messages and marching orders relayed by radio from an offshore American submarine. From the towns, covert observers had informed him and other members of the resistance throughout the province. Early in the afternoon, his guerillas came down from the mountain in full view.

They converged at the entrance to the goathole and formed a relay of men disgorging the military equipment from the cave onto the waiting carts under the watchful eye of Basilio. Our dogs milled curiously, sniffing among the throng drawn by the unfamiliar scent of gun oil and the metallic smell of thousands of bullets in their shiny brass shells—blunt nosed, pointed, and larger shells meant for the fifty-caliber machine guns.

In a few hours, the weapons would be distributed to the hundreds of guerillas in the outlying towns inland and across the river. They had been waiting for this particular moment. We watched from the window of the house until dark. In the morning, the yard was empty and had been swept clean, bereft of any evidence of the previous day's activity.

211

The Landing

As a tide ebbs and flows, now the roles were reversed. The fallen Titan, America, reeling from the calamitous bombing of its ships docked at Pearl Harbor, further saddled by its engagement in the war in Europe against Germany, had recovered from its losses and was now the aggressor. It sent its newly assembled planes, tanks, and overwhelming manpower into the final showdown against the Japanese army.

In the Philippines, General MacArthur kept his promise: he returned.

Two and a half months after the US forces invaded Leyte Island in the middle of the Philippine archipelago, those of us living in the island of Luzon received an early warning.

It came from the sky. In January 1945, at mid-morning, thousands of silvery white particles came floating down.

Aunt Mari and I were out at the time at the edge of the woods looking for mushrooms. Restive after an hour of futile searching, I glanced up. Shouting urgently, I pointed to the sky.

Mari stood, cupping her hands on each side of her face for a better look. A favorable gust of wind wafted paper leaflets toward us.

Mari snatched one out of mid-air, read it, and exclaimed, "The American soldiers are back!"

Over the years, I still remember the lines on the message.

"Make way for the fighting men. I have returned. Douglas MacArthur"

In Bisal, the atmosphere was jubilant, but it belied the tension beneath the surface as families worried for the safety of the able-bodied men who were to put themselves in harm's way once again.

Captain Toribio's guerillas, fully armed, yet keeping a respectful distance like a pack of wolves on their prey, came nipping at the heels of the retreating Japanese. They were part of a concert of guerillas awaiting their cue from the conductor's baton, who in this case was the commanding general of the US forces landing at the Gulf of Lingayen in Luzon.

Toribio's mind was awhirl with anticipation. The enemy was going to get away while he was shackled with orders to allow the enemy to withdraw. His men were chomping at the bit; their clenched jaws and focused expressions demanded a chance at retribution for what they had endured and the men and loved ones whom they had lost. What could they do?

He surveyed in his mind the lay of the land around him, and thought of the back roads and backwaters through which he and his men had shuttled through in their clandestine trips stashing caches of war supplies.

Toribio gathered his men. Standing on a tree stump so he could be seen by everyone, he bared his thoughts and asked for their opinions. It was Basilio who came through with a plan. All nodded in agreement and set to work.

With little rest, they went down the back trails and took a shortcut with the hope they would reach a point in the road before the Japanese column. Along the way, they exhorted hundreds of local townspeople to join them.

They were in luck. Upon the arrival of Toribio's men, the Japanese column hadn't passed. In fact it would be at least a day away. The roads were serpentine, going around forests, fast-moving streams, and immoveable boulders of stone. Moreover, the roads were so rocky that an ill-advised increase in speed by the vehicles carrying loads of men and pulling heavy weapons behind them could lead to a blown tire or a broken truck suspension.

Around the headwaters of the Agno River, various inlets and sidestreams converged. In the planting season, local farmers and fishermen used a system of dams and paddies to control the level of water in the rice fields and fish pens where they raised and sold thousands of silvery cichlid fish called *bangus*. This body of water stretched for miles. At some points, the ponds and pens came close to a well-traveled dirt road. If this road became inundated, it would slow the path of the retreating Japanese.

The civilians in the area were roused from their homes; armed with shovels and mattock picks, they broke up sections of the dams and paddies. For good measure, they dammed a portion of the Agno River.

Thus diverted, a vigorous flood of water broke through like an abscess gathering momentum. Within hours, the road was flooded. To their pleasant surprise, the whole road stretching more than a mile was invisible beneath the rushing muddy water teeming with fish.

Basilio pointed out the fork in the road used by the local folk as a detour leading up the hills, a narrower path but passable for one vehicle to get through at a time, an alternate route the enemy soldiers would have no choice but to take. Here they could wait for the Japanese column to pass and set up an ambush.

When Toribio quizzed the local menfolk about the detour, many voices spoke in unison. The local elder spoke above the din. He knew what they were looking for. It was only half a mile down the path, but it had a ravine on one side. Toribio positioned his men and waited.

The Japanese commander, sword sheathed at his waist and leather leggings dusty with grime, stood on the hood of his command car and surveyed the flooded road ahead. He thought it was unusual since it wasn't the rainy season. In front of him, his lead captain sent men on foot to check out their options. Two soldiers waded in the flooded road. A length of rope attached to a spool on the front of the lead vehicle was tied around each man's waist. Two tugs on the rope would signal they had reached dry land.

The ankle-deep water began to reach their knees. Four hundred feet farther, their boots sucked up the brown mud, slowing down their forward progress. They began to tire with the effort but kept moving. At the midpoint the water started to swirl. Occasional dead brush floated by. They tried to get a line of sight of the road ahead, but the road beneath them had made a slight curve. One of the men made a wrong move, blundered beyond the edge of the covered dirt road, and stepped into the mucky rice paddy. The quicksand effect of the mud was unable to sustain his weight, and his head swiftly disappeared beneath the water.

The other soldier kept going. The humility of failing was too great. He never made it to safety either.

Through his field glasses, the Japanese commander saw the two soldiers disappear beneath the water. He instantly ordered the rope cut and considered Plan B. He evaluated the area, pointed to the fork in the road, and turned the column toward it.

Toribio's pulse raced when he received the signal that the Japanese had taken the bait. An hour later, he heard the creak and whine of engine motors and unoiled hinges of trucks coming in his direction. He was now a seasoned veteran of war, but it still gave him that anticipatory lust for danger and the rush of uncertainty that in this battle he could either live or die.

The chosen ground was a narrow bend in the road around a large protruding rock against the hillside. On one side was a shallow ravine fifty feet down and strewn with small boulders. The old man at the village had pointed out to Captain Toribio's men the perfect place for an ambush.

215

Toribio assigned three snipers above the rock well covered from view. They were to fire no more than one clip apiece upon the leading enemy officer in the convoy, then withdraw. A third of his men were to hide in the boulders below, then fire for about five minutes, allowing time for the snipers to come down, take cover, or withdraw. The rest of the men were to cover the withdrawal of the ambush party.

His plan was to delay the enemy's advance before the landing of the main battle force of the Americans at Lingayen Gulf. The guerillas did not have the manpower or firepower to vanquish the Japanese fighting force they were facing. Nip and tuck would have to do.

To a degree, the plan worked. The snipers killed the soldier manning the machine gun on its swiveled turret, but missed the commanding officer standing close by. Three Japanese soldiers marching alongside were instantly killed in the opening volley. The enemy column was rooted in place for another two hours, wary of any further attacks, while Toribio's men slinked away to find another target of opportunity. His men hoped the delay in the defensive forces of the Japanese would buy precious time for the advancing American army to wade ashore and save some lives at the very least.

On a "light overcast, dappled pre-dawn sky," as a historian recorded it, the American forces commenced a pre-assault bombardment at seven o'clock from the sea at Lingayen Gulf, eighty kilometers from my hometown.

From the air, squadrons of American fighter aircraft with five-cornered white stars on their fuselages and wings were sent aloft. Waiting to do battle against them was a vastly outnumbered Japanese air force signified by the large round red zero painted on them.

A free-for-all dogfight ensued, the circle of the fighting arena in the air ever enlarging as the protagonists sought room to maneuver in the deadly dance of death.

On the ground one hour later, one-hundred-and-seventy-five-thousand men made a beachhead landing over a twenty-mile-wide swath on the shores of Gulf of Lingayen not far from Bisal.

I was an unplanned witness of the air battle that took place on that momentous day.

Kites and Dogfights

When it came to kite flying, the earthen dike along the river was a perfect venue. The winds glanced off its sloping sides to launch the frail bodies made of strips of bamboo and bright colored paper.

That day in early January 1945, the wind lifted our kites taut on their restraining strings against the skies. Playing out the string to bare spool, they remained aloft with nary a dip or a slide to either side. Finding little need to tend to them, we anchored the kites to wild shrubs.

We sat on the grass conversing idly, feeling quite comfortable under the mid-morning sun and the cool breeze.

To my left sat Benny, eyes closed, not saying a word.

Next to him, Filo was telling the story about the tantalizingly beautiful marble owned by Alfie, an older boy who said he would exchange it for Filo's two rubber bands. Following the trade, the marble broke apart in Filo's hand. It had a crack in it and was held together with spit. But Filo's used rubber bands were slightly frayed, so in hindsight, it was an even swap.

In the distance, I could see our herd of goats grazing greedily as if they were eating the last blade of grass.

Then a thought came to me. "The guavas in our backyard should be ripe by now."

Benny's eyes opened. Almost in unison, we scrambled to our feet.

We left the kites to their own devices and were now in a mad scramble to reach the guava grove first. We climbed our favorite tree

218

with the alacrity of a troop of hungry monkeys, abandoning caution, trusting the supple branches to support us.

We had no pockets, so we stuck our shirt bottoms inside the waists of our short pants and stuffed the fruit into the front of our shirts.

Benny was unafraid of heights, so he always went for the tallest of trees. Spotting a ripe guava at the highest branch, he started upward, grabbing a tenuous limb for support.

He saw movement above.

Too high to be flying birds.

"Look over there! Airplanes!"

In the sector of the sky visible to us, there were dozens of them, all flying in different directions: Japanese planes with red circles versus the American planes with five-cornered white stars on their wings and fuselages.

In the heat of the battle, there were no drawn lines.

It resembled a free for all in a bar brawl: one threw a punch while the other parried. Sometimes an enemy plane was right next to an American plane, but neither pilot needed to be concerned of the other—each was focused in attacking someone else. As the adversary broke away or was vanquished, the victor locked in on a new target.

The planes silvery bodies glinted as they reflected the rays of the sun. They resembled flying crosses against the background of blue sky. As they took turns becoming the pursued or the pursuer, they jockeyed to face each other head-on like two bulls trying to lock horns.

We beheld flits of light from bullets fired off their noses just beyond the propellers followed by the delayed rat-tat-tat-tat of their machine guns reaching our ears. Each of the combatants refused to cede ground to evade a head-on collision until the last moment in a deadly game of chicken.

Like a troupe of performers on a revolving stage, another group of protagonists replaced them, filling the sky. The characters were different. Their motives were the same: kill the enemy.

We clambered down the trees and laid on our backs on a pile of freshly threshed rice stalks. Nonchalantly, we bit on a guava like children eating popcorn while watching a television show.

My favorite warplane on that particular day was the American P38 fighter with the double fuselage. Like a game cock, it seemed to be more nimble and feisty than the Japanese Zero.

The pitch of the engines changed from angry roars to whines of protest as the pilots pushed their planes beyond their limits. They dove, twisted in random directions, and jinked desperately to save their planes and themselves from the bullets fired by the pursuers.

An American pilot nosed his plane almost vertically skyward in a last-ditch effort to elude an enemy fighter on his tail. The straining machine proved equal to the task, sending the plane upward, giving its all like a spirited steed climbing a steep hill.

Finally spent of its power, the engine stalled. The pilot turned the nose of the plane straight down. The momentum of gravity re-started the engine. Now he was the hound chasing the hare.

The fighter pilot trained his machine guns at his pursuer, taking advantage of his new-found speed from the momentum of the dive.

The plane below, a Japanese Zero, had no choice. It dipped to avoid the line of fire from the American fighter, then turned tail and tried to escape.

The Zero did not see another plane coming broadside at him until the last second.

Reflexively, he abruptly changed course again—right into the gun sights of the American fighter who followed doggedly from behind, matching his prey's every twist and turn.

The two protagonists disappeared from the center stage in the sky. We focused our attention to the other dogfights above us.

An American Mustang with its signature thunderous growl suddenly came out of nowhere from almost treetop level following an enemy airplane that appeared to have taken a mortal hit.

They were the same dueling planes we had watched in the sky. Smoke was coming out from one wing of the enemy plane.

Through the open cockpit, I caught a quick glimpse of the Japanese pilot. A white bandana stained with soot was wrapped around his forehead. He was struggling in vain to maintain control. The plane wailed a high-pitched groaning dirge as it spiraled with a trail of dark smoke to the ground below, ending with a final boom.

Behind and slightly above, the Mustang followed in hot pursuit, the American pilot's drawn pale face in profile, looking scared. Noticing that the burning Zero fighter was going to crash, the Mustang veered away, clawed for the safety of the sky, and was gone.

On that impromptu show staged in the sky that day, many lives and planes were lost from both sides. Mostly it was the outnumbered Japanese. The dogfights finished as fast as they had begun. Benny, Filo, and I rose to retrieve our kites in time for lunch.

The next morning we scanned the sky but saw no activity. Three days later, hundreds of American planes flew in V-formation upon formation, silvery wings aglint, unopposed in an endless procession, which lasted for at least two hours. They filled the air with the magnified sound of buzzing insects.

Their destination: Bataan, Corregidor, Manila, and points south. The Liberation from the Japanese was finally at hand.

When General Douglas MacArthur returned to the Philippines, he landed his main force in the island of Leyte, located at the "waist" of the Philippine archipelago. In doing so, he moved his forces south and north, dividing the enemy resistance. He was opposed by a division-size force of 250,000 Japanese soldiers

221

cobbled by General Yamashita from Chinese Manchuria and Korea. Sixty-thousand Japanese troops came from the island of Luzon to the North. A fierce battle ensued lasting two months with over 60,000 Japanese soldiers killed and 3,000 Filipino guerillas and American casualties. This did not impede the advance of the allied forces to their final objective: Manila.

To lay the groundwork for the push to Luzon and Manila, MacArthur rapidly established landing fields for the Air Force in the island of Mindoro, located southwest of Luzon, a move which General Yamashita did not anticipate.

The hundreds of planes in procession that I witnessed from my backyard likely came from this island.

Having won the decisive Battle of the Philippine Sea that effectively destroyed the main battle fleet of the Japanese Navy, the American Navy was free to prowl the Philippine waters in the weeks that followed, bombing Japanese ships that carried food and other supplies. This ultimately starved the 250,000 Japanese troops in Luzon and other key islands of the Philippines.

The Withdrawal

With a superior military force of American and Filipino guerillas hounding them, the Japanese army was now on the run. It was their turn to deal with no obtainable reinforcements to replace their casualties and replenish dwindling supplies.

This was the seminal moment that Tirso was waiting for. Upon hearing the news about the landing of MacArthur's forces, he came down the mountain to join the first band of guerillas he encountered.

General Yamashita had hoped the fertile rice belt of the central plains of Luzon Island would serve as a lifeline to feed his troops, but the growing bands of guerillas that Tirso joined gave them no respite, pressuring them, denying access to the rice granaries.

Given time, the better armed and battle-hardened Japanese could have easily overcome this recalcitrant band of Filipinos, but they had to keep moving to higher ground or risk the chance of getting cut off from their retreating comrades. Additionally, the pressure of the American troops landing in increasing numbers was becoming too much to bear. Slowly, they gave ground. It was their turn to deal with the inevitable. With their chance at resupply cut off, the Japanese troops became like a man caught in the death embrace of a giant python.

When the much-awaited arrival of the liberating forces of the US Army came to the vicinity, Tirso's band joined the American forces on the march southward to liberate other towns along the way, until they came to the outskirts of the city of Manila.

The Japanese Admirals

Of great significance were Japanese losses of many of its key military leaders in the final chapter of the war. Among them: Admirals Yamamoto, Koga, and Fukudome.

Admiral Isaroku Yamamoto: Architect of the bombing of Pearl Harbor. Planner of the unsuccessful attempt to finish off the remainder of the American battle ships at Midway Island. Cut his teeth as a junior naval officer by specializing in guns and cannon warfare. Envisioning the future role of air power with the discovery of the airplane, he switched his interest to bombs carried in military aircraft. Commander in Chief of Japanese forces stationed in the Pacific. Nicknamed "80 sen" by the Tokyo geisha girls who manicured his eight fingernails—he lost two fingers from an earlier conflict in the war against the Russians.

How he died: A Japanese message was intercepted by the Americans. It mentioned that Admiral Yamamoto planned to inspect firsthand the battlefront somewhere in the Solomon Islands. The coded message was specific as to the time and place. On that fateful day at 6 p.m., he changed his uniform from the navy white to camouflage to honor the land-based army units he would be visiting, and boarded an airplane with heavy escorts. Two squadrons of American warplanes hid in the clouds and carried extra gas tanks. They hoped that the intelligence received was accurate and that the predicted time to intercept Yamamoto's plane was correct. The planes only carried enough fuel to remain aloft and get the job done in a short period of time before returning to the safety of the carriers.

The glint of the wingtips of the unwary Japanese escorts finally came into view. The American planes came swooping down, homing in on Yamamoto's aircraft and his escorts in a fiery surprise ambush. Riddled with multiple shots, the admiral's plane crashed into the jungle below. Yamamoto was found, seated with his Japanese sword grasped in one hand, by Japanese searchers. He had died before impact with a shattered jaw and major shoulder injury.

Admiral Koga: Three days later, Japanese Fleet Admiral Mineichi Koga, stationed at Palau Island, was chosen to replace the deceased Admiral Yamamoto. The Americans were closing in, taking island after island. The situation had become desperate.

Koga crafted the "Z Plan." It outlined an all-out throw of the dice of all Japanese assets: men, ships, and planes at a certain time and place of its choosing against America.

If Japan were to emerge as the victor, it might have forced America to concede to a truce and allowed the former to keep the Empire it had carved in the Far East. He presented his plan in person before the war cabinet. Tokyo approved. Koga returned to Palau to implement his plans; however, the situation had become tenuous. The American fleet with its 535 ships, 15 carriers, 900 planes, and 127,000 troops was forging ahead slowly against Koga's remaining assets of 6 carriers, 450 planes, and the land-based troops embedded in various islands.

Admiral Koga ordered his staff to move central command headquarters from Palau Island to Davao, six hundred miles northwest on the island of Mindanao in the southern Philippines. They boarded three aircraft. The first held Admiral Mineichi Koga and his staff. Accompanied by twelve junior officers, Admiral Fukudome, Koga's second in command, carried the "Z" documents on the second plane. On board the third aircraft were the radio and signals team.

A fierce tropical *taifun* caught them enroute. The plane carrying Admiral Koga crashed into the sea leaving no survivors.

Admiral Fukudome in the second plane, noting ample fuel, directed his pilot to skirt the typhoon's path and head for Manila farther north. But the winds were unrelenting. They buffeted the frail craft, enabling little headway. The pilot was extremely capable but tired from battling to keep his aircraft aloft. He checked his dials and map and advised Admiral Fukudome that he was aborting the plan to head north. He started his descent to the nearest landfall at Cebu Island a few miles to his west. They were in the teeth of the wind. The plane's nose refused to level out. Air pockets gave them a bumpy ride. One moment they were up by fifty feet, and in a split second, they were down by a hundred. Fukudome looked out and saw the mountainous waves of the angry ocean lashing against the window panes. They were going to crash! Fukudome, as left seat pilot, announced he had the plane and took over the controls, willing the plane to head skyward. But he overcorrected.

Fukudome Survived.

It was April Fool's Day, 1944. His aircraft had gone down; it floated half submerged in the water. In the melee to exit, Fukudome grabbed a seat as a flotation device, hugged it to his chest, and jumped out the open cockpit door into a yawning maw between two giant waves. His head disappeared beneath the water. He kicked to come up for air and winced; his leg must have been badly injured. Concentrating on survival, he tightened his floating jacket around him. A few yards away, heads bobbed in the water on a huge wave. They did not see Fukudome. These junior officers, younger and more fit, had managed to stay together. The storm had passed, the waves had not abated, but the current was taking them closer to shore. They clung to one another for warmth. To keep their morale up and remain awake, one started singing a familiar song. Everyone joined in.

Two friends were beachcombing. After a *taifun*, who knew what could be found stranded on the beach? They heard singing.

Shading their eyes against the sun, they saw the outlines of heads in the water. They paddled out in separate *bancas* toward the floundering figures. When they came close, they realized the men in the water were Japanese soldiers. The two stopped short of helping the men into the boats, because the beachcombers were frightened. But they could not leave the soldiers to drown even if they were the enemy. One jumped off his *banca* and climbed into the boat with his friend. Together they rowed back to shore. The Japanese managed to gain control of the abandoned *banca* and also reached the shore. Guerillas had been alerted and awaited the soldiers.

The Japanese became hostages to a thousand-strong unit of Filipino and American guerillas led by an American civilian mining engineer, Colonel Cushing. A few days later, Admiral Fukudome was rescued by local fishermen. Cushing's men returned to the beach to get him. Fukudome's injuries were severe and he had a bad infection. The guerillas treated him for his injuries. Fukudome fought to maintain his focus in spite of his delirium and did not reveal his true name and rank as a leading flag officer of the Japanese military. He hoped his fellow hostages would keep the secret to themselves as well.

The guerillas radioed for instructions. They had hostages. What should they do? Intelligence officers on the network locally and all the way to MacArthur's headquarters in Brisbane, Australia would not comment. What would be derived from taking mere soldiers for questioning? Besides, the American submarines, busy with other duties, would be placed at risk if they tried to smuggle the hostages out.

Forty-eight hours after the typhoon and plane crash, Japanese planes were abuzz, scouting the hills and shores. The local Japanese commander sent soldiers from town to town, looking for Admiral Fukudome and his staff. This was in response to the report from two survivors of the Fukudome party who had found their way to the Japanese garrison in Cebu. Frustrated by the non-cooperative civilians, he ordered radical measures. Hundreds were wantonly killed in every town and barrio.

Cushing moved deep into the forest with twenty-five men and hostages. They took turns carrying Fukudome in a makeshift stretcher and continued to care for his wounds. They retrieved leaflets dropped from Japanese aircraft demanding the return of the hostages. There was no response from the civilians and the guerillas. To sweeten the deal, the Japanese dropped more leaflets. This time, there was a reward of fifty-thousand pesos equivalent to twenty-five-thousand dollars. Otherwise, the killing of civilians would continue. Cushing radioed again for instructions. He received noncommittal replies.

In the interim, there was another development at a nearby beach. A barrio native saw something shining in the water a mile away. He walked to a neighbor's house who confirmed something was out there. Treasure perhaps? They paddled together to find a red packet entangled in seaweed covered with slime and oil. They recalled other floating boxes that the Japanese retrieved on the shores of the island. What were they looking for? Might this be it? Was there an unseen eye observing them from ashore at this very moment?

Now more cautious and fearful, they lifted the object from the water, placed it in the bottom of the boat, and concealed it with a fisherman's net. They anchored the boat a hundred yards off the beach and swam back to shore. The packet would remain there until they had a plan.

The Japanese soldiers swooped down on the barrio the next day in a lightning raid. They searched every house and ground, but not the *banca*. The two friends were now certain that they had something important in their possession. They retrieved and opened the package. In the glow of the oil lamp inside their hut, they discovered a thick sheaf of papers matted by water seepage and conspicuously marked with a red "Z." And gold coins. The temptation was great. They buried the coins and had a heated discussion. They finally decided to turn over the whole package and its contents to the guerillas. The risk to their families if the Japanese found out would have been a colossal and tragic mistake.

The next communiqué from Cushing now piqued the interest of MacArthur's staff. Captured hostages, cash reward, and the "Z" packet. Hmm. The reply was urgent. Send them over. A submarine would hover offshore and receive the packet and the hostages. It would take a few days. A Filipino guerilla, Colonel Abcede, and his men, would be the conduit for the transfer.

Cushing, meanwhile, could not wait any longer. He had already arranged a temporary truce with the Japanese a few days earlier. He would return the hostages if there was no further killing of civilians. The Japanese agreed. They also agreed to a temporary truce not to pursue Cushing and his men for medically treating Admiral Fukudome, even though they still did not know his identity at the time. Only the "Z" packet, stuffed inside an empty cannon shell, was given to Colonel Abcede's unit who in turn handed it to the commander of the waiting American submarine.

Millitary historians think the contents of the "Z" plan—the breaking of the Japanese codes and signals contained within—changed the outcome of the war in the Pacific and the Philippines. MacArthur's plan to liberate the Philippines from the south at Mindanao was probably altered because of the document's contents. Instead, he changed the invasion plans to land in Leyte, bisecting the Philippines at a vulnerable point. The decisive naval victory in the Battle of the Philippine Sea was also probably influenced by the contents of the Japanese playbook that planned to lure the American navy to fight closer to the Philippine coastline, where Japanese guns facing seaward could attack them.

Yamashita.

Commanding General of the Japanese forces in the Philippines, Tamoyoki Yamashita, ordered the main body of the Japanese force three-hundred-thousand strong under his command to the Cordillera Mountains, on the highest mountain peak north of Central Luzon, where he planned to make a final stand.

It wasn't easy. They were ascending narrow trails that led to jungle and hard uneven terrain. But he was thinking shrewdly. If he was having difficulties climbing the mountain, so would his adversaries in pursuit. At the bends in the roads and trails, he laid out traps of cannons and machine guns, which were getting too heavy to lug farther. Monsoon season was about to come upon them. The muddy clay of the mountain trod upon by countless feet would slow down hunter and the hunted. The rest of the men were randomly scattered in hidden pockets all over the large mountain, so in order to extricate them, it would take a long process. Delaying the enemy advance was exactly Yamashita's purpose. In fact, his plan allowed him to resist the pressure from American and Philippine forces until the formal surrender of Japan in 1945.

Yamashita was credited for the swift takeover of Malaya and Singapore. On December 8, 1941, one day after the surprise bombing of Pearl Harbor, he marched into Singapore and Malaya with little opposition. Thirteen-thousand British soldiers surrendered, the largest number of British to ever submit to any foreign power.

His unorthodox approach was devious and brilliant. He camouflaged his primary intent by infiltrating the lush jungles of

Vietnam and Thailand from the north with troops trained in jungle warfare and survival. When the Japanese army emerged, he provided them with bicycles to travel on the foot trails and backroads, thus bypassing the sea route that would be noisy and obvious as to where he was going. Along the route of advance and inside Singapore and Malaya, he had spies who felt the pulse and gauged the reactions of the British. The British were aware of the Thailand invasion by the Japanese but were reluctant to transgress into a foreign territory because it might be misconstrued as land grabbing on their part. When they realized Japan's intention for Singapore, it was too late. The British had anticipated any attack to come from the sea and were heavily prepared for such a contingency, not a threat from inland. This masterful victory earned Yamashita the sobriquet, "The Tiger of Malaya."

Yamashita earned accolades in the military and high political circles in Japan. Many felt he should replace the current leader in this critical phase of aggression against America and the rest of the world.

Prime Minister of Japan, Hideki Tojo, the man he was supposed to supplant, would have none of that. In a pre-emptive move, Tojo ordered Yamashita to a remote posting at Manchuria away from the battlefront.

In October 1944, when the tide of the war was already tilting against Japan, Yamashita was called on to do the impossible— assume command of the Japanese forces in the Philippines and perform a miracle. They wanted him to win a game of poker with the bad hand already dealt before him. The Americans were wresting island after island in the Pacific area away from the Japanese.

Ultimately, he invoked young Japanese pilots to *kamikaze* attacks into the ships of the Americans "for the glory of the Emperor." The response was extemporaneous. There were many volunteers, but there were only so many planes to expend. In the end, it was all to no avail. The American and Filipino forces swept over the Japanese resistance. Enemy supplies of food and war material were cut off from the sea, starving the army of Yamashita. With the fall of their air and naval capabilities, the Japanese land forces became highly vulnerable. The next move for the allied forces was to invade Luzon and retake Corregidor and Bataan. Manila would be next.

Manila: The Defense and Invasion

To cover the withdrawal of the main Japanese forces toward the mountains, General Yamashita assigned a rear guard of fifteen thousand men under the command of a naval officer, Admiral Iwabuchi. His orders: defend Manila, delay the advance of American and Filipino forces trying to retake the city, withdraw and join the main battle force in the northern mountains of Luzon.

Iwabuchi felt deeply honored at being chosen. Two years prior, he had the misfortune of losing his main battleship, *Kirishima,* in the Battle of Guadalcanal. He had misgivings that as its captain, he should have gone down with his ship. Here now lay an opportunity to redeem himself.

Iwabuchi's force of sixteen thousand were mostly navy men. A fifth were army soldiers. Like the regiment of American and Filipino soldiers who defended Corregidor three years earlier, they were a mélange of men whose ships had been sunk, men at the navy yard, and a lesser assortment of men from other army units. They used familiar weapons: anti-aircraft naval weapons salvaged from disabled ships off Manila Bay, a few rockets that made a deafening noise, which was demoralizing but effective. They had no tank or air support and no training in urban warfare, hence no close combat weapons.

Pre-war Manila, roughly five miles long and five miles wide, was populated by one million inhabitants. The city grew from the north and south banks of the Pasig River as it emptied into Manila Bay. Most of the houses of the time were bamboo roofed with thatched nipa palm. A few, owned by the very affluent, mostly

233

foreigners, were concrete and wood homes, some air-conditioned. Six major bridges connected the river banks. On the North bank from the bay area inland were the warehouses and piers, business, and residential districts in that order. On the South bank at the mouth of the river, Fort Santiago guarded the bay. The fort sat within *Intramuros* (the Walled City), which was enclosed by over a mile of nearly triangular, eight-foot-thick, twenty-foot-high wall. A mile east on the north bank lay Malacanang Palace, home of the Philippine President.

Newer concrete buildings south of *Intramuros* had recently been erected to house the legislative, agricultural, and post office buildings. The fabled five-star Manila Hotel overlooked the bay. General Douglas MacArthur had a six-room suite, which is named in his honor even to this day.

Iwabuchi laid mines to booby-trap most of the main street thoroughfares. Small cannons stripped from disabled naval ships provided covering fire at the intersections. All bridges were rigged with explosives. As the offensive forces advanced, these were to be blown up. The reinforced concrete government buildings, less vulnerable to artillery, served as defensive forts. Admiral Iwabuchi chose one building, the agriculture department office south of the Pasig River, for his central command headquarters. Fort Santiago, inside *Intramuros* with a river moat on the south, was the centerpiece of the defense with cannons, rockets, and anti-aircraft guns.

The American and Filipino offensive plan was to encircle the Japanese by land from the north and east and south. West of Iwabuch's command center was Manila Bay. Under special orders from General MacArthur, the liberating forces withheld the use of air power or artillery for fear of endangering the lives of the innocent civilians and destruction of historical buildings. However, this proved to be costly. American and Filipino soldiers died in numbers as the Japanese refused to yield. The Japanese naval anti-aircraft guns proved as effective and as lethal on land-based targets.

There were small gains inside the city of Manila. The Filipino guerillas came out of hiding and harassed the enemy from within. They cut telephone lines, rendering communications between Japanese units useless. By radio, they provided the American soldiers with the locations of pillboxes, ammunition dumps, fortifications, troops, information about buildings and bridges being prepared for demolition.

After days of considerable delay, American artillery was finally allowed. Bombs fell on Japanese strongholds, but they also caused widespread conflagrations to the flammable nipa-thatched homes in the residential districts, killing or injuring many civilians.

17-Manila streetfighting

The Japanese fought with a vengeance. The reinforced concrete buildings south of the Pasig River became fortresses. They

---

[8] By Keystone, Getty Images—https://www.gettyimages.com

blew up stairwells and dropped grenades from the upper stories, in effect signaling they were committed to fight to the last man. Some lashed themselves to their posts with rope so they would not falter and run. The Americans countered with flamethrowers aimed through the blown holes on the walls and roofs wrought by incoming artillery.

On the streets, the enraged Japanese went on a rampage, shooting civilians of every sex and age. They raped the women. Hostages were used as human shields in the shrinking pocket of Manila available to them within the walls of *Intramuros*.

Seventy years later after the war, a woman then thirteen years of age, recalled how her family was fired upon by Japanese soldiers with machine guns as they fled for cover inside the city. Her younger sibling, two years of age, fell wounded. A soldier chased after them. Having failed, he speared the fallen baby with his bayonet. Her parents survived the war. Her father, Elpidio Quirino, went on to become President of the Philippines between 1948-1953.

The advancing Americans and guerillas from the north slowly made headway. After weeks of hand-to-hand fighting and house-by-house searches, they finally reached the riverbank, but they had to pause—the bridges had been blown up. An initial attempt to cross the one-hundred-sixty-foot-wide river in rubber rafts by soldiers using rifle butts for paddles was successful; further attempts along the river led to casualties from Japanese fire. Eventually, a slim foothold on the opposite bank was secured. The army's engineers hastily built a pontoon bridge. Soldiers, tanks, and trucks crossed at last.

Bizarre things happened. Civilians walked nonchalantly from the opposite direction to cross the bridge to get out of harm's way. The befuddled soldiers could only pause as the civilians shook the hands of their liberators, unmindful of the whizzing bullets. Amazingly, only a few civilians were killed in the crossfire, but the elated Filipinos did not blame the Americans. Some remained alongside the liberating troops to point out where Japanese soldiers were entrenched.

Following in the wake of the liberators, despicable human vultures, well-organized bands of Filipino civilians, looted anything of value from the liberated homes.

Iwabuchi's pocket of resistance was rapidly shrinking. His superiors offered him an opportunity to withdraw—a slim corridor to escape with his men could be kept open to the east by a Japanese unit waiting outside the tightening circle should he choose; but he did not. In a terse reply, he apologized for his incompetence and for placing so many of his men at severe risk. He also added that in his judgment, they were boxed in with no chance of escape, which left them with only one choice—to stand and fight to the last man for the glory of Japan and the Emperor.

Iwabuchi sent wave upon wave of suicide squads with mines strapped on their persons to attack, even diving beneath the tracks of the advancing American tanks. Civilians and guerillas caught within the city took the brunt of their frustration. To conserve ammunition, Japanese soldiers herded these people into homes they set afire, burning them alive.

Here are excerpts of documents referencing the battle to retake Manila from the Japanese perspective:

Diaries from various Japanese soldiers at Intramuros, Manila
- *7 February—1945 150 guerillas were disposed of tonight. I personally stabbed and killed 10*
- *8 February—Guarded over 1,164 guerillas brought in today*
- *9 February—Burned 1000 guerillas tonight*
- *13 February—On guard duty at guerilla internment camp (Fort Santiago) 10 guerillas tried to escape. They were stabbed then burned*
- *13 Feb 1945—...muddy water. Forced to dig well for drinking (Intramuros)*

- *13 Feb 1945—The enemy approaches closer. We cannot cope with the enemy's concentrated fire. The city has fallen into hand-to-hand fighting. It is estimated that the enemy is using three divisions of Americans, Australians, and Filipinos.*

Kobayashi Group Orders 13 Feb 1945—There are now several thousand Filipino guerillas inside Manila...even men and women have become guerillas...All personnel on the battlefield with the exception of Japanese soldiers and special construction units will be put to death.

Japanese War Documents Recovered Post War—Operation Order to 149th Japanese AirField Bn concerning the attackers..Aim—The Battalion will strictly conceal its plan, and, after annihilating guerillas in front of the positions occupied by Section—units with one blow by night attack, will...burn native villagers.

MNDF Central Operations (Ultra Secret) Feb 15, 1945 Japan Army—The City has fallen into hand-to-hand fighting..This unit will make plans for suicide attack...wounded will be made to commit suicide...materials will be burned...every man will attack until he achieves a glorious death. Not even one man must become a prisoner. Friends of the wounded will make them commit suicide.

Personnel will be lightly garbed and carry as much ammunition as is possible.

When Filipinos are to be killed, they must be gathered in one place and disposed of to conserve manpower and ammunition. Because disposal of dead bodies is troublesome, they should be gathered in houses to be burned or demolished...they should also be thrown in the river.

The fighting lasted almost two months from February to March 1945. There was no formal surrender. Before taking his own life, Iwabuchi said to his staff, "If anyone has the courage to escape, please do so. If not, please take your lives here." He closed the door to his room and blew himself up with a hand grenade.

History blames Iwabuchi for disobeying the orders given by his commanding officer. General Yamashita chose to surrender rather than kill himself so that no one else would take the blame. Yamashita was condemned to die following a contentious postwar trial that went all the way to the US Supreme Court. On the night of his hanging, clad in the ordinary garb of a prisoner and preceded by a Buddhist monk chanting prayers, he was led to the hastily assembled gallows outside of Manila. To the end, he disavowed his guilt on the charge of murder of Manila's many civilians. He prayed for his parents, children, and, finally, for the honor of the Japanese Emperor. Another item rankles in the history notes. Why was a naval officer chosen to take over a military operation that was on land where no ships of war were involved?

Is it possible that Yamashita selected Iwabuchi to defend Manila in the waning years of the war so that he could redeem his honor by dying in battle?

Wounded Japanese soldiers chose to die rather than surrender to the advancing USAFFE soldiers. In Corregidor, at Malinta tunnel, there is a section where Japanese soldiers blew themselves up or killed themselves with their swords or knives rather than surrender. Many jumped off the cliffs of Corregidor to their deaths.[9]

As the outcome became obvious, the retreating Japanese in the Philippines were given a second option by their superiors: melt into the hills, forests, and mountains, ride out the war; and await the

---

[9] War Plan Orange-Wikipedia. www.history.army.mil/books wikipedia.org, Bataan Death March-World War II. History.com, Wikipedia.org/Battle of Corregidor/Gibraltar of the East, Wikipedia.org/Corregidor#Geology

order from the Emperor when to come down and fight again. These soldiers were ordered "not to die by their own hand."

Some did.

Saito was one of those few. He had been chosen by his immediate superior, a non-commisioned officer, Sergeant Oshi, to come with him along with two others.

It was a high honor he could not refuse. Packing bare essentials in anticipation of a long and arduous journey, they made haste to leave.

In a fleeting moment of unmilitary gesture, their commanding officer appeared to wish them well with a faint flicker of softening in his usually stern demeanor. These men had fought valiantly with him and wished he could keep them, but the fortunes of war were turning in a direction that was beyond his ability to control. He told them that a lone armored truck and a squad of soldiers were on their way to an outpost heading up the mountain. Why not hitch a ride as far as they wished until they could get off somewhere to reduce the chance of detection from prying eyes?

Several kilometers later, they slid off the still-moving truck as they came to the edge of thick jungle and melted silently into the brush. They found a footpath but chose to avoid it; for now they were no longer the predators. Sergeant Oshi laid out a plan to head in the direction of a bare-face cliff close to the summit of the mountain. They moved at a dogtrot, taking advantage of the still-flat ground.

They came to an abrupt clearing, where the dying rays of the afternoon sun reflected against water in the reedy marsh ahead. Suddenly, Oshi heard a sloshing sound and motioned everybody down. They retreated into the shadow of the trees and waited. A water buffalo emerged from the belly-deep water snapping fallen twigs in its path with ponderous hooves. Its head moved from side to side catching a last meal of grass. Astride its broad back was the owner, a peasant in his bare feet, who urged his mount left, right, or forward with gentle tugs on a short rope attached to a ring and bolt that pierced the sensitive septum of the animal's nostrils. One persistent pull meant a left turn; two gentle tugs meant a right.

Once the water buffalo and its rider had passed, Oshi and his men moved on, knowing the danger of detection was still at hand. They traveled a few kilometers more before finding a place to set up camp before sunset. A half hour later, everything was pitch black.

They munched silently on their rations; each man took his turn as sentry during the night. Over the next few days the terrain became hilly. They were still in the forest, which meant birds and animals—a source of fresh meat and water—would be available.

Finally, they came to their first objective, the base of the bare rock face. Were they now in a secure place, or should they venture to the summit? If they went higher, how would they get there?

Oshi noted a line of stunted, gnarled, green shrubs along a vertical hairline split in the rock face leading to the mountain summit, which with proper foot and handholds could offer an almost vertical ascent to the top. Once there, they could scout the landscape below for enemy threats coming their way from any direction.

There were three minor problems. They had no climbing experience, not enough rope was available for safety, and Oshi was afraid of heights.

He told his men to break for a few minutes, while his eyes roamed restlessly. From their vantage point, he could see rice paddies in the distant valley—like irregular patchy squares of quilt the color of mud, rectangles and squares edged by green lines of grass growing in the partition of earth that dammed the water to sustain the rice plants. He redirected his gaze toward the rock fault and followed the line to the bottom. A silvery gleam of a falling drop of water caught his attention.

He rose for a closer look at the foot of the cliff. Hidden in a depression were dense green shrubs, which meant water. It was the last month of the dry season of 1945 and yet there was a dampness to the earth and lushness in the surrounding vegetation.

Pressing his face against the rock, he licked at the faint trickle of water and judged it fresh and potable. It wasn't much, but with a little patience and ingenuity, he could have enough to slake their thirst and then some. Unsheathing his bayonet, he scored a series of converging lines in the moist rock downward to a protruding ledge.

Several minutes later, he was rewarded with a constant fast drip of cold clear water they eagerly collected in their canteens. He continued to follow the shrubbery to his left and was surprised to see an opening shrouded in the cliff leading into a cave that appeared to lead downward. During the rainy season, a torrent of water from the higher elevation drained in this direction.

Cautiously, he descended. It wasn't much of a decline in the ground but it led to yawning hole of darkness. He looked at the ten-foot ceiling and made a decision to set up camp. He returned to the group of men and informed them of his discovery.

That night Saito had a dream about his homeland. He was trudging in the familiar landscape behind his father's home on a hillside blurred by blue haze from the mist of falling rain that softened the features of the trees and leaves. He awakened to the faint patter of raindrops on the pine needles about his feet. He shivered and pulled his army blanket over his military uniform around him. He had taken off his boots and his toes felt cold. He heard the screeching and flapping of wings above his head and held up one hand as if to ward off a blow.

Silhouetted against the dimly lit sky was a large hole in the dark cave. Thousands of flying bats raced from the two-hundred-foot ceiling studded with stalactites in a deeper recess of the cave. They would be traveling for miles in search of food, only to return before daybreak. They excreted urine and fecal droppings on the inert forms of the sleeping men. That morning over breakfast, Saito told the men what he had seen. Sergeant Oshi realized that they would need to keep moving to find a better spot.

Palawan Atrocities

Resembling the shape of a pencil-thin half moustache on a man's upper lip, the island of Palawan lies Southwest of Manila and is bounded on the west by the South China Sea.

"In December 14, 1944, one-hundred-and-fifty American prisoners of war were brutally massacred at Puerto Princesa, Palawan." Many of these POWS were survivors of the Death March from Bataan and Corregidor.

"They were forced into air-raid dugouts, drenched in gasoline, and burned. Hand grenades were thrown in and men shot or bayoneted if they tried to crawl out."

Wartime orders stated: (Intercepted Japanese cables giving orders before the advance of American troops)

a) destroy POWs individually or in groups, with mass bombing, poisonous smoke, poisons, drowning, decapitation…as the situation dictated…

b) …not to allow the escape of a single one, to annihilate and leave no traces.

How do we know?

There are physical evidences of the massacre: charred remains and burned dugouts verified by archaeological digs after the war.

There are also eyewitness accounts from those who escaped and survived.[1011]

---

[10] Palawan Massacre American Prisoners of War at Palawan/HistoryNet.com, Palawan massacre-Wikipedia.com
[11]

Sergeant Powell was one of the lucky few who were physically unscathed, owing to his assignment as telecom operator inside the command headquarters at Malinta tunnel in Corregidor. Following the surrender, he was locked up at the Bilibid correctional facility along with thousands of POWS.

A year following the surrender of Bataan, the Japanese, in need of laborers, culled out able-bodied men from the prisoner list. Sergeant Powell found himself on a short boat ride to the island of Palawan, where the enemy was developing an airfield. The work was hard and back-breaking. Trees had to be cut, boulders removed and a landing strip leveled by chipping at coral rock. It was an arduous process with mattocks and shovels, the only available tools. There was the risk of malaria from hungry mosquitos that infested the surrounding jungle. Many of the men fell ill.

On that fateful day of December 14, Powell's work gang was assigned to the edge of the jungle under the watchful eyes of two Japanese guards. He stood erect, pausing to rest briefly to mop sweat from his face, when he noted an unusual flurry of activity by the soldiers at the main camp a thousand feet away. An air raid alarm was triggered; the POWs were herded into shallow dugout shelters covered with camouflage netting, but there were no airplanes overhead. Being that they had no radio, the soldiers watching Powell's work gang were momentarily distracted and did not know what to do.

It was 1944 and the Americans were closing in to reclaim the Philippines. An urgent communiqué was received at Palawan camp from an offshore Japanese submarine. The message said, "Kill all prisoners now."

Powell noted that the guards by the main camp had set up machine guns aimed toward the prisoners. Armed Japanese soldiers carrying gasoline cans scurried from the supply depot. Suddenly, there were bursts of machine gun fire aimed at a blazing pit of cornered, helpless men. Men aflame tried to claw themselves out of the pit, only to be prodded back in and shot. Grenades were thrown in for good measure. The smell of burning flesh and cries of anguish filled the stifling humid air of the jungle.

Powell sensed imminent danger and reacted instinctively. He and a few others ran for the nearby woods. The sentries fired with their single-shot bolt-action rifles, and several fleeing men were killed; others scattered in different directions, unharmed. Some dove off the cliff into the sea and swam to an island five miles away, where friendly inhabitants and guerillas hid them in the hills.

The Japanese turned to the remainder of the prisoners, who stood rooted in a paralysis of fear and gunned them down where they stood.

Powell crashed through brush and boulders and never stopped until his lungs seemed to burst. His face was covered with blood from a violent head-on collision with a tree trunk, leaving a flap of skin hanging from his forehead to below his right ear.

An hour later, he stopped. There was only silence, broken by a faint constant chirp from a bird. Powell kept moving from the direction of the camp and climbed a steep hill, its dirt floor covered by ankle deep brown leaves and rotting wood. He scanned the gaps in the trees and saw a brown thatched grass hut.

A farmer in his working clothes, wide-brimmed straw hat, bolo in hand, was working on a clearing of land with his wife when Powell staggered toward them. Powell's skeletal appearance with the bloodied face and shirt contrasted with his pale complexion. The surprised couple let out a sigh of relief and broke into a welcoming grin. They had heard that the Americans were returning, but this seemed unexpectedly early.

Powell hid in the jungle where he was hunted by random patrols of Japanese. Within the first week following his escape, one of the soldiers walked perilously close to his hiding place; in desperation he burrowed himself deep beside an anthill and covered his body with twigs and leaves. Hours later, he felt safe enough to emerge, but at a price—his entire face and body were covered with a thousand ant bites. His testimony to the horrors at Palawan after the war was helpful in bringing light to the Japanese atrocities committed.

Diary of a Japanese sergeant 14 Dec 1944—Due to the sudden change of situation, 150 POWs were executed.... They died a pitiful death. ...I will not hear the familiar greeting "Good morning, Sergeant Major" from the prisoners who worked hard in the repair shops.

Excerpts of trial proceedings in 1948 reconstructing the Palawan Massacre following the end of the war:

In 1952, the remains of 123 victims were exhumed and moved to a mass grave at Jefferson Barracks National Cemetery near St. Louis, Missouri...And in 2009 a monument to the victims and survivors of the massacre was erected at Palawan. [12]

---

[12] Palawan Massacre American Prisoners of War at Palawan/HistoryNet.com, Palawan massacre-Wikipedia.com

University of Santo Tomas Campus, Manila

American tanks lumbered amid the rubble of destroyed buildings on either side of them. Although the rest of Manila was still in Japanese hands, this task force had to slog on, casualties notwithstanding. This was a special battle group. Its top mission: liberate the prisoners of war interned at the University of Santo Tomas before the Japanese soldiers had a chance to annihilate them.

Barricades and minefields had been set at the crossroads of the main thoroughfares by the Japanese, making expeditious passage treacherous. Enemy machine guns and small cannons manned by dug-in Japanese soldiers guarded the intersections. Somehow, the tank brigade and infantrymen trailing behind got through. It was February 6, 1945, roughly one week into the battle to retake Manila from the Japanese.

The tank commander, guided by Filipino guerillas, saw a block-long concrete wall ahead that had been intentionally spared from shelling by American artillery. Upon command, the lead tank veered sharply off the street and jumped the curb. Repeated butting attempts broke down a section of the fifteen-foot-high brick and mortar wall of the campus and hospital of the University of Santo Tomas, where sick and injured American forces from the battle of Bataan and Corregidor were interned.

As a precaution, the tanks had purposefully bypassed the main entrance with the closed iron gates in case they were booby-trapped with mines. They rumbled abreast into a large field where before the war commencement exercises for the University students

247

normally took place. The soldiers, alert for any signs of enemy resistance, crouched behind protective tanks.

The grounds were eerily deserted. Suddenly, tanks and infantrymen received a hail of enemy fire from one of the outlying buildings once used as classrooms.

The liberating forces, not wanting the Japanese defenders to start shooting the internees they had come to set free, held their fire. A loudspeaker from one of the American tanks came to life, calmly persuading the enemy to surrender.

In the tense atmosphere, the broadcast was constantly repeated. After what seemed like interminable hours of waiting, thirty soldiers emerged, empty hands in the air. They were workers of Chinese descent from the island of Chinese Formosa conscripted by the Japanese to work in the Manila shipyards. They pointed to a building where enemy soldiers charged with guarding the compound were holed up.

The Japanese commander refused to surrender. Negotiations lasted till the next day; the Americans waited patiently as long as there was no further shooting. Finally, an offer was given that was mutually satisfactory: the Japanese would not kill any of the internees. In return, the Japanese soldiers would be allowed to leave the campus with their weapons to fight the war still raging outside the campus.

It was February, 1945. One month later, the battle for the remainder of Manila would be over in favor of the liberating forces.

The Americans looked about them and were aghast, revulsed at the sight of those they had come to liberate, a sea of white faces, three-thousand-five-hundred of them, war prisoners all.

They were generally emaciated. Their facial features were like death masks. When they grinned, they exposed swollen gums ravaged by scurvy, teeth yellowed or missing. Skinny arms exaggerated their macabre appearances. Many had developed beriberi, a vitamin deficiency that swelled the legs. They were barely able to stand up, much less walk. A parchment of skin devoid of any fat covered the ribs over their pulsating hearts, their abdomens flat, almost pursed around their spine.

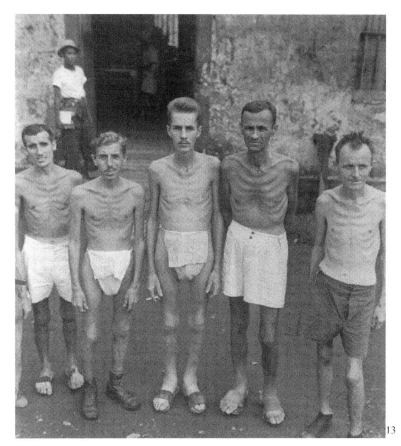

18-Liberated American POWs

Without supplies to feed the Japanese army and keep its soldiers in fighting trim, food resources had been diverted from the internment camps around the country and the hospitals. The POWs had been on a starvation diet for months.

---

[13] By Bettmann, Getty Images—https://www.gettyimages.com

At the onset of the surrender of the Philippines to the Japanese in 1942, each POW received the equivalent of a fistful of boiled rice per day. Now, rations had been reduced severely to half a cup of rice, boiled as *lugao* or rice gruel, which translates to 120 grams or 480 calories per day

For purposes of comparison, a sedentary individual by dietary standards would require 2000 calories per day just to maintain body weight and continue activities of daily living. Many never made it.

Compassionate GIs doled out food, gum, and cigarettes from the supply packs. Many of the liberated prisoners wolfed down their food only to pay the terrible price of stomach cramps, tenesmus, diarrhea, and vomiting from not having eaten for so long. The food supply of the liberating soldiers at UST was all but gone within two days, because they did not factor in having to feed the internees.

Elsewhere in Manila, two Japanese soldiers banged on Marcial's door. When he stuck out his head, he was unceremoniously cuffed and kneed before being marched into the street and watched by the Filipino traitor who had betrayed him. Joining a group of civilians who had been rounded up, Marcial was slapped, and struck with rifle butts. When he groaned, a despicable gesture of cowardice, Marcial was ultimately decapitated. The others were beaten first, then shot or stabbed.

Marcial, who chose to stay in Manila to guard the house against opportunistic looters, made a mistake that cost him his life.

In the aftermath of the massacre and the shelling of Manila, one-hundred-thousand out of a million civilians perished. For comparison, deaths from the atomic bombs dropped at Nagasaki: 38,000—80,000; Hiroshima 90,000—146,000 casualties.

American soldiers killed in action, Battle of Manila Feb 1945: 1,000; Wounded 5,000. Japanese casualties: 16,000.

In 1944, facing a manpower shortage, POWs were sent to Japan in freight ships to work in the mines and other jobs that would serve the war effort.

The holds of such ships, averaging a thousand square feet, were crammed with a thousand prisoners without adequate ventilation.

Men who got to the holds last were the lucky ones because they had the advantage of light from the open hatch and had first dibs at the food that was lowered to them at mealtime.

While they waited for the ship to sail with no breeze, it became a hot, stinking oven.

The bathroom facility was right where one was standing or sitting.

These freighters were unmarked. Many were mistaken as transport ships for Japanese soldiers and sunk by US submarines or strafed and bombed by American planes as they sailed enroute to Japan.[14]

Radio Corpsman Kehaya was in one such ship. Nothing was ever heard of his whereabouts, as with many others who probably perished during the ocean journey.

At Bilibid prison in Manila, thousands of Filipino and American POWs lived alongside hardcore criminals in cramped, squalid quarters with up to six sharing a two-bunk cell. Then they heard the creaking of the main gate and the cautious entry of liberating American troops. The rousing welcome from the imprisoned half-starved POWs was deafening.[15]

---

[14] American POWs of Japan.blogspot.com/_Palawan-massacre
[15] Battle of Manila. Wikipedia.org/wiki/

19-Orphaned Filipino Child
Around his neck, someone had written on cardboard,
"I am an orphan. My father fought and died in Bataan.
Help!"

---

[16] By FPG, Getty Images—https://www.gettyimages.com

The Liberation

It was 1945, almost a year of war, if one considers the time starting from the day of the landing to take back the Philippines from Japan. Or it would have been four years from the time of the first hostilities on the homeland in 1941 when Japan attacked.

The Filipino guerillas now came back to their respective towns and cities. They started to exact their revenge on the Filipinos who had turned into collaborators during the Japanese occupation. They were not hard to find. The civilian population pointed them out and even if they weren't identified, they were easy to spot, because they were well fed and better nourished.

And the cycle went its way, a repeat: the killing and man's inhumanity against another man. Revenge. More killing.

All to what purpose? What was accomplished?

Did the plight of mankind get any better?

At first, it sounded like a faint howling in the wind as a harbinger of an approaching rainstorm; then it became a faint rumble. It was coming from the east, in mid-afternoon. We had never heard anything like this.

It shook our flimsy bamboo and palm house like an earthquake. We stayed where we were, not moving, ears primed, ready for flight.

A chorus of shouts!

People came running past our house in the direction of the growing sound.

I stood next to Dida, my sister, her restraining hand on my shoulder. Cautiously, we allowed ourselves to be swept by the excited throng but ventured no farther than the crossroads of the dirt path from the house with the main street.

Looking to our left, we saw a cloud of dust and several tall machines larger and more menacing than anything that I had ever seen. The sound of their creaking wheels and loud engines shook the ground in our little town. They came single file in the narrow main street meant to accommodate horse-drawn vehicles. Their metal tracks chewed up the short strip of asphalted road along the school and town hall.

Seated atop an open turret was a soldier with a very long antenna behind him that seemed to sprout over his helmeted head. On the tank's front was a five cornered white star I had seen in the airplane dogfights from our backyard with Benny and my friends.

Americans!

Marching alongside the tanks were tired soldiers on foot, their rifles slung on straps over their shoulders, a sign there was no threat ahead of them.

On the left was a Filipino soldier dressed in army issue one-size-fits-all khakis rolled up at the sleeves, baggy over his small frame. The stride looked familiar, a rifle slung by a belt across his chest. He looked exhausted, dirty, and grimy. He panned the crowd, spotted me, and grinned in my direction.

My father!

On the other side of the moving tank a man rode a horse. I recognized the horse before the rider. It was Kerlat! And Captain Toribio. He had been met on the outskirts of Bisal by Bolol, who now walked alongside him in bare feet and peasant clothing looking like the faithful Sancho Panza of Don Quixote fame. Local guerillas, finally home from the war, walked alongside the tanks, followed by American soldiers.

The commander of the outfit had been prescient enough to give the local guerillas the honor of entering the town first. Tay ran ahead. He directed the people to open the iron gates to the schoolhouse. Entering the principal's office, he produced two flags. The column of soldiers and tanks entered the schoolyard.

Tay rang the school bell. The townspeople lined up in neat rows and sections like schoolchildren around the flagpole, placing their right hands over their left breasts. The American flag was raised to the singing of God Bless America, followed by the raising of the familiar tri-colored flag of the Philippines and the singing of the Philippine National Anthem.

Before we left, Dida and I milled around a tank, atop which a GI kept repeating a coded message on the radio, "Bring down banana tree," which must have meant something, but I did not care.

I was more interested in the pieces of Dentyne gum he was distributing to the children with his free hand. Dida, being the taller, managed to catch one of them. We split it between us.

It was my first taste of gum—ever.

On the way home, Dida asked, "What did you do with your gum?"

"I swallowed it."

I could see the disbelief in her face. "You are only supposed to chew it. Now your intestines will stick together."

I did not sleep well that night as I waited to die.

But I didn't and I'm glad. If I had died, who would be around to write this story?

How I Remember Noli, My Brother

He was born in May, 1942, a month after the surrender of Bataan to the Japanese Army.

He came in the night. Upon waking one morning, I found a baby cozied up in a soft flannel blanket in the adjacent bedroom. Only his face showed, traces of waxy film from dried amniotic fluid on his cheeks, slits for eyes, lips pursed, nuzzled against Mother's breast.

Noli's hands were gloved in a square of cloth the size of teabags pursed with a string around his tiny wrists to protect his face from his fingernails.

Where did he come from?

From that day on, I lost my standing as the main focus of attention in the family. That night, I slept in an adjoining bedroom next to my father. Noli had taken my place next to Nay so that he could be nursed on demand during the night.

I was hidden behind the open door leading to the next room in a game of hide and seek. I could see him through the crack between the hinges. His eyes seemed riveted in my direction, saliva drooled down his lower lip onto his already wet bib.

Game over. He had found me.

As I came out of my hiding place, it seemed he had lost interest in the game.

He now crawled toward the nearby arm of the sofa. Taking a vise grip with his tiny fingers, he clawed himself to a standing position. Swiveling his head, he espied the coffee table and headed for it in two tottering steps.

I watched in dreaded anticipation: he was going to bang his head against the table's edge! But no! His extended hands grabbed the table's side and he managed to remain erect. Victorious, he let out a coo, gurgling a fresh stream of saliva down his chin in celebration.

I had just witnessed Noli taking his first walk!

Noli was on the bed on his back as if sound asleep, eyes closed. His right arm and hand rose and fell every few seconds making a rhythmic chopping tap on the thin reed mat.

Noli lay motionless, on his back, eyelids partly open. It was as if he were peeking.

He was face up inside an open box lined with baby-blue silk. His fine, dark hair was neatly combed and parted to each side, head rested on a silken baby pillow.

He wore a short-sleeved shirt folded once at the arms, and light-green plaid short pants with the front bib reaching to the front of his chest.

I noticed the white and brown shoes.

Everything he wore used to be mine. I had already outgrown them.

A stranger lifted me in his arms so I could see Noli from an adult's perspective. He softly whispered words for me to say.

"I will miss you, my brother," I repeated after him. And the lid of the coffin closed.

I remember asking this kind man, "What is this place?" That strange place with boxed shapes and large crosses, high walls, and a large forbidding door.

"We are in a cemetery."

I asked myself a silent question that was left unanswered. *What is a cemetery?*

Finally, the man put me down to stand beside my mother.

My mother wore a black dress, a black veil over her head and face. There was silence, broken by the muted sound of grieving.

I heard a drip, like the slow patter of water. I looked at the sky. There was no rain, only an occasional fluffy white cloud.

A sob. I saw mother's tears cascading down her cheeks, unchecked. The falling teardrops made a splattering sound on the parched brown leaf by her feet. She made no attempt to dab her face. The dainty, doily-sized handkerchief in her hand was already saturated, useless.

My mind now took me back to that day as I sat on the threshold of our granary, Noli's bones in a thin box rested on my lap.

Born 1942. Died 1944.

Counting back the years, I was three-and-a-half-years old when I first received the gift to be able to remember.

I am humbled by the discovery. How awesome is the gift of human intellect!

What Happened to Noli?

He was standing atop a bed set close to an open, unbarred window of our home. He had leaned out too far looking for a pet rabbit that had hidden beneath a tea shrub in the fenced garden.

In one fleeting second, Noli had fallen headlong from fifteen feet to the ground below. There was no visible sign of external injury. He never regained consciousness.

The next question is tough, because it seems incriminatory and irrelevant. Who was babysitting? Different answers: one of my aunts, an older sister. My mother.

A few years ago, as a much older person, I could not resist asking my oldest sister, already in her early eighties, just to set the record straight. There was a faint sadness in her eyes, a subtle change in her affect. Immediately, I regretted my lack of tact in bringing up a topic that had been layered with scabs over the years to hide the tragic death of a loved one.

But she said "Mother was."

I looked away, pensive. My memory took me back to the moaning, recurring nightmares of Nay over the years until her passing. Was there a correlation to this ghost of her past?

The Bureau of Graves wrote my family a letter, to wit: "The statute requires that a body buried ten years has to be exhumed if the annual fee is not paid; and the remains re-interred ...in a lesser space." My parents, who had then moved to a faraway town, elected to bring Noli along with us.

In 1957, Noli's remains were permanently interred in my father's hometown at his family's gravesite.

Epilogue

Bai, my grandmother, passed away thirty years after the war at the ripe old age of eighty-seven. Although she could hardly read or write, her ten grandchildren venerated her for her loving ways, comforting presence, and sage words of advice.

My mother, Nay, taught all grade levels in the elementary school until her retirement at the age of sixty. She died peacefully at the age of ninety-two. Her mind remained clear and lucid till the very end.

During her last few days, I asked what she remembered best about her career. She replied, "Teaching home economics to young girls on how to sew and cook."

In 1948, she received an invitation to be the commencement speaker at a fashion school Convocation founded by one of her students.

One of our last conversations drifted back to the onset of the war. She recalled her moments of doubt about getting Nora and me home, because she also carried a personal physical burden: in her womb, a four-month baby, my brother, Noli.

Tay joined the Philippine Army as Captain of Infantry between 1943 and 1945. His unit was assigned to Bayombong, Nueva Vizcaya, where they pursued the retreating Japanese of General Yamashita up the mountains of Kiangan, Mountain Province. Following the formal surrender of the Japanese, Tay went back to teach in the public school system. He advanced in the school hierarchy to school principal, then school supervisor.

Because of his potential, he was sent to India under a UNESCO grant for further studies. Returning home, he taught at local colleges and eventually became a school superintendent.

Captain Toribio's stature rose as a community leader and war hero. He remained well respected. Eventually, he served in various elected positions as governor of the province and as senator in congress.

Sergeant Gonzalo was killed in action in the final days of the war while engaged in mopping up operations in the mountainous terrain of Kiangan, against the withdrawing Japanese forces. He was a victim of friendly fire when his company split up in the night to outflank the enemy.

Benny, my bosom friend, became an engineer. Emigrating to America, he became involved in the hydroelectric dam projects across the country.

Japanese General Masaharu Homma, commanding the 1941 invasion of the Philippines was executed in April 3, 1946, following a war crimes trial for allowing the atrocities to happen to the allied POWS in the Bataan death march and to the men who surrendered at Corregidor.

Sergeant Oshi and his Japanese soldiers stayed in the cave for a few months and had learned to live off the meat of trapped live bats, augmenting their diet with wild vegetables, fruits, and small animals caught in the nearby jungle. Saito used his fishnet-making skills to find vines they stripped lengthwise into long strings and made a lattice on an oval frame like outsized butterfly nets. Using ten-footlong bamboo handles, they waited at dawn to snare a few of the thousands of fruit bats returning from the jungle where they had feasted on ripe fruit they found in the dark—an uncanny display of their night vision and sensitive smell of ripened fruit from miles away. Before daybreak, they were back at the cave, suspended by their hooked claws over the cavern ceiling, to rest and sleep till nighttime.

Months passed into years. The war was over, but Oshi and his men still clung to their infinite faith that their Emperor would let them know when to come out of hiding to fight again. Surely, with the awesome armed might of the Japanese Imperial Army and Navy they had seen firsthand before they left the shores of Japan, it wouldn't be much longer before they received orders for them to rejoin their comrades to finish the war.

Patience and faith was the key. The call would come. Oshi and his men were sure.

The year was 1955. The sentry on watch poked the sleeping form of Sergeant Oshi. They could hear the sound of engines and the booming echo of crashing trees. Sighting with his field glasses, he saw ant-like figures of men wearing yellow jackets and hardhats, unarmed, on bulldozers felling trees for timber and to build a road.

Sergeant Oshi felt a nervous churning inside his stomach. Years back they had explored farther down and deep into the recesses of the cave, but the darkness and fear of stepping into an abyss led them to procrastinate. Now the tipping point had been reached. An escape route must be found. Discovery of their presence was not an option.

Lighting bundled dry sticks for torches, they explored the deeper recesses of the cave with a sense of urgency more than ever before. In advance of what would be a final departure out of the bat cave, they stashed food provisions at intervals on flat shelves of rock on the cave walls along the way. There was no time to get waylaid or sidetracked.

The cave ran for several miles. They noted puddles of clear potable water that filtered along the wall or dripped from the ceiling. Thus, their water supply would not be a problem. At a point they noticed a trifurcation. They elected to follow the largest opening. The men noticed that the walls funneled down several hundred feet ahead.

At the far end, there was a final opening, a two-feet-high by four-feet-wide slit on the floor, covered by water a foot deep. Dismayed, Oshi was about to retrace his steps. Saito tarried, sat on his haunches, and beamed his torch close to the opening. The light flickered and waved.

"There is an air vent beyond!" he yelled. He took off his clothes, backpack, and rifle, then tied a length of rope to his left ankle. By the time the men returned, Saito had disappeared; the only sign of him was the wiggling rope trailing behind. Twenty feet of rope length later, Sergeant Oshi felt three sharp tugs on the rope in his hand, a pre-arranged signal that all was well. The rest of the men followed.

Saito had emerged into a large cavern with cathedral ceilings. The spectacle caused by torch light bouncing off glasslike stalactites from the roof resembled hanging candles on candelabra. The multiple facets shining like polished diamonds held him in awe. Directly beneath the tips of the overhanging stalactites were stalagmites, upright stalks of crystal of varying heights rooted in the floor. When the other men joined Saito with their torches, the visual display was further enhanced. Stalagmites gleamed like multi-colored jewels—yellow, green, blue, ochre, opal caused by crystalized minerals of copper, cobalt, magnesium, and sulfur that had mixed with the dripping water and crusted into the mounds of iridescent beauty over thousands of years.

Ahead was a pool of limpid water, clean and inviting, that emptied silently in the dark corner of the cavern into a vanishing edge. On the other side of the pool, a triangular shape like a smudge seemed recessed against the white rock wall. Curious, Saito waded across for a closer look. He was astonished to discover a large imbedded conch shell, proof that these mile-high mountains emerged from the ocean floor to become the Philippine archipelago.

The soldier uneducated in geology could only scratch his head. He thought someone who had been there before him must have planted it there as a prank to vex the next explorer who came along.

They had not yet found the location of the air vent, but were encouraged by the progress made thus far. Tomorrow they would resume the search. For the time being they shed their clothes to take a long-needed, leisurely bath, cavorting like children splashing in the pool and having fun.

In 1967, twenty two years after the end of the war, a Japanese soldier's body was brought to the police station in the town of Bisal on a makeshift bamboo stretcher.

Farmers living at the foot of the mountain shot him trying to steal a pig in its pen in the middle of the night. He was dressed in tattered but many times mended uniform of a Japanese soldier.

An Arisaka rifle and rounds of ammunition laid across his chest. A mess kit lay next to him, the top open. It contained a sweet yellow yam, already peeled and cut in large cubes ready for cooking. On the side of the mess kit were Japanese scrawled letterings and the etched markings of a fish spine of Saito, the fish scaler.

The stories of Japanese soldiers who hid in the jungles and mountains in the Philippines awaiting the order of the Emperor of Japan to fight again are well documented. In 1974 thirty years after the war, a soldier named Onoda, refused attempts by leaflets and loudspeaker broadcasts to come out of hiding. It took a Japanese citizen to persuade him with a letter from his former commanding officer who had survived, telling him that the war was over. He had carefully preserved his cap, uniform, and rifle, which was in working condition. One such soldier upon returning to Japan, finding suburban living untenable after years in the jungle, moved to South America and founded a jungle-survival school.[17]

---

17 The WWII soldier who hid in the Philippine Jungle for 29 years. Filip.Know/2/05/2014

The Dogs: "Go Ahead. Take Them All"

Every uttered word sounded like an explosive shot from a gun fired close to my ears. I flinched uncontrollably.

My little cupped hands could not contain the torrent of my tears that flowed as I lay face down on my damp pillow and tried to stifle the sound of my sobbing.

Five men were seated around the coffee table with Tay in the covered balcony, their somber expressions faintly illuminated by the solitary oil lamp in their midst.

They had arrived in the early evening. Their conversation was subdued, deferential, and respectful to my father. They were talking about our five dogs. Earlier in the day, a pregnant woman walked by on the dirt road in front of the house. The dogs barked, but did not leave the fenced yard.

The woman apparently became intimidated, panicked, and ran. Probably triggered by a primeval instinct, Betty, our lead dog, bounded over the fence, followed by the others, and gave chase.

The woman started yelling and flailing her arms. One of the dogs nipped at her extended hand which, led to further screaming.

As a rule, the dogs held their prey at bay and did not attack unless commanded to do so. This time they went berserk, tearing at the hem of her long dress and nipping at her exposed legs.

Thus, the visit by these men, one of whom was the husband. The other was the barrio elder who did most of the talking, not irate, but in a calm and measured voice.

They were not asking for compensation, nor were they requesting medical treatment. Between polite quaffs of the *basi* offered by Tay to each man, the spokesman suggested that the dogs should be taken away in light of the fact that it was deemed as a bad omen for a pregnant woman to be hurt just before the harvest season; the spirits must be appeased.

In all fairness, these were simple folk, farmers all, honest but superstitious. Tay considered the safety of his family, should he disagree with their line of reasoning. Sadly, he agreed.

Three days later, scattered ashes from a bonfire were seen a few kilometers alongside the river where the dogs were killed.

I thought of the brown long-haired dog looking very fierce, yet so loving and protective of me, the dog named Betty, our five dogs, our early warning system, defenders of our home twenty-four hours a day, protectors of our chickens from marauding monitor lizards, indefatigable, all of them taken away, forever.

-o-

Kerlat, the irrepressible stallion that he was, caught the fancy of Lino, a young man, scion of a prominent family in town. Don Toribio had been fending overtures of Lino's interest in purchasing the horse for years. But the Don, now mired in politics, long sessions, and meetings, could no longer indulge Kerlat with the spirited sprints and gallops, and the attention which he craved.

Reluctantly, he caved in.

Lino trained Kerlat to prance and canter in an unnatural measured way by tying all his four legs with rope for months. Looking at his eyes and the way he tossed his head against the reins as his new master rode him around town, I could only guess that *Kerlat* was not happy.

20-Llamido St., named for Bayani
Photo taken by Felix in 1990

-o-

In the year 2000, a street in Bayani's hometown was named in his honor by a town council proclamation. It runs parallel to the main street leading to the town market.

To this day, each year on December 30, Bayani's birthday is celebrated by his loved ones. Bayani, which means "hero" in my language, had fulfilled his destiny. Framed on the living room wall of his parents' home for all to see are his medals for courage, valor, and sacrifice.

-o-

"Give me ten thousand Filipino soldiers and I shall conquer the world."

General Douglas MacArthur

This may seem like hyperbole, but knowing the Filipino mentality, I would tend to personally agree. Once committed to loyalty, given proper training and the right equipment, which, alas, was not afforded in the years before World War II, a Filipino in that generation would not hesitate to stand and fight to his last breath for the proper moral cause under the right leader who could cajole them into battle. The documented battle exploits of the Philippine Expedition Force in the Battle of Korea with properly trained troops in the 1950's will attest to their courage and determination to stand firm in the face of overwhelming odds.

References

1. War Plan Orange—Wikipedia. www.history.army.mil/books wikipedia.org

2. Bataan Death March—Wikipedia.com

3. Bataan Death March—World War II. History.com

4. Bataan Death March—1942-Eyewitness. History.com/Bataandeathmarch

5. Bataan Death March—WWII/Brittanica.com

6. Bataan Death March/Atomic Heritage— www.atomicheritage.com/history/Bataan death-march

7. American Experience.MacArthur—Capture and Death March/PBS. www.Pbs.org/wgbh/amex/macarthur/sfeatures/bataan-Capture.html

8. Palawan Massacre—American Prisoners of War at Palawan/HistoryNet.com

9. Palawan massacre—Wikipedia.com

10. American POWs of Japan—blogspot.com/_Palawan-massacre

11. Japanese occupation of the Philippines—Wikipedia.org

12. Philippine Resistance Against Japan—Wikipedia.org

13. The Battle for the Recapture of Corregidor—Seizure of Malinta Hill/Aftermath. Wikipedia.org

14. Battle of Manila—Wikipedia.org/wiki/

15. The WWII soldier who hid in the Philippine Jungle for 29 years—Filip.Know/2/05/2014

16. General Masaharu Homma— www.Pacific War.org.av/ Japanese War Crimes/Ten War Crimes/Bataan Death March

17. War Stories between my father and former comrades-in-arms in our home after the War

18. Wikipedia.org/Battle of Corregidor/Gibraltar of the East

19. Wikipedia.org/Corregidor#Geology

20. Marine Corps Gazette. November 1946. The Fourth Marines of Corregidor

21. The Siege and Capture of Corregidor. HyperWar:History of USMC Operations in WWII,vol.1,Part IV,Chapter 4

22. Japanese Accounts of the Battle of Manila. Ricardo Trota Jose.

23. General Tomoyuki Yamashita—Nathaniel Helms. Feb 1996. World War II Magazine

24. How Filipinos Helped Defeat the Japanese. FilipiKnow.com

25. Z Plan Story—www.Nationalarchives.gov

26. Z Plan Story by Greg Bradsher. Fall 2005.vol37 no.3 Prologue Magazine

27. General Tomoyuki—Yamashita/HistoryNet

28. The New Military History: Jonathan Wainwright

29. Mineichi Koga/World War II Database

30. World War II in the Philippines—A timeline-latimes

31. Battle of Corregidor—Wikipedia

32. The Limahong Invasion—Cesar V. Callanta. 1989

33. The Battle of Manila—Thomas Huber/
    battleofmanila.org/Huber

34. The story of Li-ma-hong and his failed attempt to conquer
    Manila in 1574—Kahimyang.com/kauswagen/articles/1319

35. US Army in WW2—The War in the Pacific. The Fall of the
    Philippines. Louis Morton

Made in the USA
Middletown, DE
26 August 2019